AN AMERICAN FEDERATION OF TEACHERS BIBLIOGRAPHY

AN AMERICAN FEDERATION OF TEACHERS BIBLIOGRAPHY

Compiled by
Archives of Labor and Urban Affairs
Wayne State University

Wayne State University Press
Detroit, 1980

Library of Congress Cataloging in Publication Data
Wayne State University, Detroit. Archives of
    Labor and Urban Affairs.
    An American Federation of Teachers bibliography.
    Includes index.
    1. Teachers' unions—United States—Bibliography.
2. Academic freedom—United States—Bibliography.
3. American Federation of Teachers—Bibliography.
I. Title.
Z5815.U5W38 1980 [LB2844.53.U6] 016.33188'113711'00973
ISBN 0-8143-1659-X   80-13142
ISBN 0-8143-1660-3 (pbk.)

CONTENTS

Preface   7
Acknowledgments   9
Abbreviations   11

I.   BOOKS   13
General Surveys   15
Treatment of Particular Issues   16

II.   ARTICLES   29
Before 1920   31
1920–1929   44
1930–1941   59
1942–1949   80
1950–1959   89
1960–1965   100
1966–1969   118
1970–1979   143

III.   DISSERTATIONS AND THESES   183

IV.   SELECTED AFT DOCUMENTS
      AND PAMPHLETS   191
Before 1960   193
1960–1969   196
1970–1978   200

V.   ARCHIVAL MATERIAL   205
Archives of Labor and Urban Affairs, WSU   207
Other Repositories   213

Index   217

Founded in 1916, the American Federation of Teachers has played a vital role in the development of modern American education. Union contributions toward better salaries, professional recognition for teachers, and improved schools have been immeasurable. AFT members have taken the lead in a wide range of educational concerns including classroom discipline, selection of textbooks, the use of television, and funding. The AFT has also been at the forefront in such areas of general interest as civil rights, political action, and social and economic reform. *An American Federation of Teachers Bibliography* is a guide to sources for this dynamic history of the union and covers the development and activities of the AFT from the founding of the earliest locals through June, 1979.

The scope and purpose of the bibliography is twofold. First, it provides a wide selection of readily available materials, primarily articles, books, and pamphlets, for those interested in AFT teacher unionism and the role of the union in American education. Secondly, it lists references to other items, such as AFT documents, reports and position papers, dissertations and theses, and manuscript collections, for the researcher who is seeking additional reading or is interested in doing more extensive study.

The bibliography is divided into five separate divisions: Books, Articles, Dissertations and Theses, Selected AFT Documents and Pamphlets, and Archival Material. The entries in the first division represent the most important published monographs on the AFT. The general books serve as introductions to the main issues in the AFT's evolution, while the specific works concern topics of a more limited nature.

The second division of citations includes articles from professional, labor, and popular journals and magazines, and covers almost all aspects of AFT growth. Arranged alphabetically within chronological divisions of approximately ten years each, these entries reflect many important and particular issues of a specific time period, e.g., the Loeb rule, "yellow-dog" contracts, Communism, educational reconstruction, civil rights, and paraprofessional organizing, as well as general union and educational developments. Since many of the articles deal with more than a single topic a subject arrangement was not feasible. It was necessary, however, to divide the nearly 1,200 entries into reasonably sized units. The division by decades accomplishes this, and serves to group the articles into significant phases of the AFT's history.

The dissertations and theses contained in the third division represent scholarly studies of particular topics relating to the AFT and its impact on education, teacher unionism, and society. The next division of entries provides a select sample of AFT documents and pamphlets. These documents were chosen because of their fundamental importance in the AFT's evolution, and also because of their ready availability to the interested researcher. The selected items represent only a small portion of the total amount of documents and pamphlets generated by the AFT, but illustrate important issues and developments in AFT history.

The last division provides a short guide to various archival and manuscript collections that relate wholly or in part to the AFT, and represents the major manuscript holdings as of June, 1979. For manuscript use and accessibility regulations the researcher should consult the relevant institution.

It was decided not to include a comprehensive index since most of the works cited, including the articles, deal with a variety of topics. Rather, a selective index of topics of general interest and major importance has been compiled by entry number.

Most of the publications listed are available in libraries throughout the United States. Some, however, are relatively rare; for information regarding their locations, researchers should consult the *National Union Catalog* or the *Union List of Serials.* Most of the doctoral dissertations listed are available on microfilm through *Dissertation Abstracts International.* A number of the AFT documents and pamphlets cited are available through the ERIC Document Reproduction Service (EDRS), P.O.B. 190, Arlington, Va. 22210.

PHILIP P. MASON, *Director*
Archives of Labor and Urban Affairs

ACKNOWLEDGMENTS

In 1969 the American Federation of Teachers designated the Archives of Labor and Urban Affairs as the official depository for the union's historical records. Since that time not only have materials been received from the headquarters of the AFT, but from several locals across the nation, and from many individuals who played a role in the growth of the organization. These papers have developed into one of the nation's finest research collections on education, unionization in education, and related topics.

It has long been felt by the staff of the Archives that in addition to this archival material, assistance was needed for those seeking information from published or other sources. The AFT generously consented to provide the funds needed to develop such a bibliography.

Many persons have participated in the preparation of the work. Special note should be made of the contributions of Donald Haynes, historian of the AFT, who developed the outline of the bibliography and gave invaluable assistance in advising the staff on pertinent entries and AFT history. Several staff members devoted long hours to the project. Paul Anderson prepared the first draft, which was subsequently revised and updated by Erwin Levold.

Joan Rabins, of the Archives staff, provided singular assistance during the final drafting of the manuscript. Jean Spang in her role of editor provided invaluable counsel. The typing of the various drafts was done by Susan Kudek and Lynne Nagy.

ABBREVIATIONS

AASA	American Association of School Administrators
AAUP	American Association of University Professors
AFL	American Federation of Labor
AFSCME	American Federation of State, County and Municipal Employees
AFT	American Federation of Teachers
CB	Collective Bargaining
CIO	Congress of Industrial Organizations
COMPAS	Comprehensive Program for American Schools
CORE	Congress of Racial Equality
CTF	Chicago Teachers Federation
CTU	Chicago Teachers Union
CUPE	Council of AFL-CIO Unions for Professional Employees
DFT	Detroit Federation of Teachers
ERIC	Educational Resources Information Center
FEA/United	Florida Education Association/United
IEA	Illinois Education Association
IFT	Illinois Federation of Teachers
MES	More Effective Schools Program
MSTA	Michigan State Teachers' Association
NEA	National Education Association
NLRB	National Labor Relations Board
NYSUT	New York State United Teachers
PEF	Public Employees Federation

PTA	Parent-Teacher Association
QuEST	Quality Educational Standards in Teaching
SUNY	State University of New York
TUCNY	Teachers Union of the City of New York
UFCT	United Federation of College Teachers
UFT	United Federation of Teachers
UUP	United University Professions
WSU	Wayne State University

I. BOOKS

1. American Federation of Teachers, Commission on Educational Reconstruction. *Organizing the Teaching Profession: The Story of the American Federation of Teachers.* Glencoe, Illinois: The Free Press, 1955. 320 pp.

    This "official history" of the AFT follows a topical, rather than a chronological, approach to union history. There are chapters concentrating on the founding of important locals, on the state federations, and on significant issues such as the fight against "yellow-dog" contracts. The work also contains a valuable appendix, with excerpts of key documents in AFT history, many of which are no longer available.

2. Braun, Robert J. *Teachers and Power: The Story of the American Federation of Teachers.* New York: Simon and Schuster, 1972. 287 pp.

    A journalistic account critical of the AFT. Following a brief review of early AFT history, the work concentrates on events of the late 1960s. Braun charges that teachers' unions may deprive the public of control of the schools.

3. Eaton, William Edward. *The American Federation of Teachers, 1916–1961: A History of the Movement.* Carbondale, Illinois: Southern Illinois University Press, 1975. 240 pp.

    Eaton argues that for over a half-century, the AFT has maintained a consistent program for the betterment of the teaching profession and the schools. The book reveals many of the organizational problems faced by a small union with membership concentrated in large cities of varying character and ethnic composition. In general, the work is well documented. Eaton ends his coverage at 1961, thus not providing an analysis of the AFT's most turbulent decade to date.

4. Robinson, Aileen W. *A Critical Evaluation of the American Federation of Teachers.* Chicago: American Federation of Teachers, 1934. 64 pp. Reprinted in *American Teacher*, 19 (October, 1934), 12–14, 16; (November–December, 1934),

7–10, 30; (January-February, 1935), 4–7; (March–April, 1935), 6–8, 13; (May–June, 1935), 6–9.

Written as a master's thesis for Smith College, this work argues that the union "is more effective with its small, vigorous group than any organization made inert and conservative by gathering to itself all the teachers."

5. Taft, Philip. *United They Teach: The Story of the United Federation of Teachers.* Los Angeles: Nash Publishing, 1974. 283 pp.

Covers the entire history of organized teachers in New York City. Taft stresses the organizational continuity from the founding of the TUCNY, Local 5 (1916), through the period of the Teachers Guild (1935–1960), to the contemporary UFT.

6. Zitron, Celia Lewis. *The New York City Teachers Union, 1916–1964: A Story of Educational and Social Commitment.* New York: Humanities Press, 1969. 288 pp.

A history of Local 5, expelled from the AFT in 1941 as Communist-oriented and later disbanded after the UFT successes of the early 1960s. The book attempts to refute charges that the local was ever dominated by subversives, emphasizing instead its dedication to academic freedom and reform. Zitron devotes scant attention to the leadership of Henry Linville and Abraham Lefkowitz, who left Local 5 in 1935 to form the rival Teachers Guild.

TREATMENT OF PARTICULAR ISSUES

7. Addams, Jane. *Twenty Years at Hull-House.* New York: Macmillan, 1910. 462 pp.

Contains an account of the CTF lawsuit for taxation of corporate properties at the turn of the century.

8. Alberty, Harold B. and Boyd H. Bode, eds. *Educational Freedom and Democracy.* Second Yearbook of the John

Dewey Society. New York: D. Appleton-Century, 1938. 292 pp.

A book of essays by noted educators on the exercise and defense of freedom in various aspects of American education. Includes "Defense of Freedom by Educational Organizations" by H. W. Tyler.

9. Alexander, Carter. *Some Present Aspects of the Work of Teachers' Voluntary Associations in the United States.* Contributions to Education, No. 36. New York: Teachers College, Columbia University, 1910. 109 pp. Reprint ed., New York: AMS Press, 1972. 103 pp.

The first comprehensive study of teachers' associations. Discusses early attempts of teachers to affiliate with the AFL and outlines the aims of the CTF, the first successful local.

10. Andree, Robert G. *Collective Negotiations: A Guide to School Board–Teacher Relations.* Lexington, Massachusetts: D. C. Heath, Heath Lexington Books, 1970. 248 pp.

A survey of the teacher representation struggle of the late 1960s, presenting the varying degree of success of the AFT in several states.

11. Axtelle, George E. and William W. Wattenberg. *Teachers for Democracy.* Fourth Yearbook of the John Dewey Society. New York: D. Appleton-Century, 1940. 412 pp.

A series of essays focusing on the theme of teaching democratic ideals. The most pertinent for AFT history is Axtelle's essay "Social Implementation of Democracy and Education," crediting the union with national leadership in the development of sounder systems of school finance and the extension of educational opportunity.

12. Beale, Howard K. *Are American Teachers Free?* New York: Charles Scribner's Sons, 1936. 885 pp.

A study of academic freedom in the 1930s, touching upon attacks by communities, school boards, and courts on the AFT and its members in the battle for recognition.

13. Bendiner, Robert. *The Politics of Schools: A Crisis of Self-Government.* New York: Harper and Row, 1969. 240 pp.

Provides a general discussion of the "teacher rebellion," plus specific information from New York City, Flint and Ecorse, Michigan.

14. Berube, Maurice R. and Marilyn Gittell, eds. *Confrontation at Ocean Hill-Brownsville: The New York School Strikes of 1968.* New York: Praeger, 1969. 340 pp.
A book of "documents" (reports, guidelines, hate literature) and partisan articles from all sides of the dispute. The UFT viewpoint is represented in articles by Eugenia Kemble and Sandra Feldman.

15. Brameld, Theodore, ed. *Workers' Education in the United States.* Fifth Yearbook of the John Dewey Society. New York: Harper and Brothers, 1941. 338 pp.
A collection of essays on the history, problems and prospects of workers' education programs. See especially the contributions by Mark Starr, George S. Counts, and Theodore Brameld. The book includes an in-depth bibliography on the subject.

16. Brinkmeier, Oria A., et al. *Inside the Organization Teacher: The Relationship Between Selected Characteristics of Teachers and Their Membership in Professional Organizations.* Danville, Illinois: Interstate Printers and Publishers, 1967. 119 pp.
This study of Minnesota teachers indicates that the state federation draws its greatest strength from male secondary school teachers and that the membership is more "tough-minded," "sophisticated," "imaginative," and "impatient" than its NEA counterpart.

17. Brooks, Thomas R. *Toil and Trouble: A History of American Labor.* Foreword by A. H. Raskin, 2nd edition, revised and enlarged. New York: Delacorte Press, 1971. 402 pp.
Briefly summarizes AFT developments of the 1960s from the historical perspective of the American labor movement.

18. Callahan, Raymond E. *Education and the Cult of Efficiency.* Chicago: University of Chicago Press, 1962. 273 pp.
Briefly discusses early AFT opposition to "efficiency" innovations which may lessen the quality of education.

19. Campbell, Roald F. and Donald H. Layton. *Policy Making For American Education*. Chicago: Midwest Administration Center, University of Chicago, 1969. 103 pp.

    Contains a description of the 1967 Detroit Federation of Teachers' strike and credits the national AFT with crucial support for the local.

20. Campbell, Roald F., et al. *The Organization and Control of American Schools*. Columbus, Ohio: Charles E. Merrill, 1965. 553 pp.

    Offers a brief review of the AFT position in the early 1960s.

21. Carlton, Patrick W. and Harold I. Goodwin. *The Collective Dilemma: Negotiations in Education*. Worthington, Ohio: Charles A. Jones, 1969. 339 pp.

    A selection of essays and articles, including Charles Cogen's "The American Federation of Teachers—Force for Change." There are numerous short references to AFT positions in other selections.

22. Carson, Sonny (Mwlina Imiri Abubadika). *The Education of Sonny Carson*. New York: W. W. Norton, 1972. 203 pp.

    An autobiography by the community relations director of Brooklyn CORE and advocate of "community control" of New York schools. The final portion of the book narrates the author's perspective of the Ocean Hill-Brownsville dispute in 1968.

23. Carter, Barbara. *Pickets, Parents and Power: The Story Behind the New York City Teachers' Strike*. New York: Citation Press, 1971. 178 pp.

    Covers events from 1966 to 1970 and includes a helpful chronology of important events. The author maintains that the UFT was "trapped" into a white-backlash position in 1968.

24. Chamberlain, Leo M. and Leslie W. Kindred. *The Teacher and School Organization*. 3rd edition. Englewood Cliffs, New Jersey: Prentice-Hall, 1958. 550 pp.

    Summarizes reasons for and against labor affiliation.

25. Childs, John L. and George S. Counts. *America, Russia and*

the Communist Party in the Postwar World. New York: John Day, 1943. 92 pp.

A publication of the AFT's Commission on Education and the Postwar World. The work outlines problems of cooperation between countries with such divergent systems as those of the US and the USSR.

26. Cole, Stephen. *The Unionization of Teachers: A Case Study of the UFT.* New York: Praeger, 1969. 245 pp.

Attempts to isolate the sociological conditions which led to the UFT successes of the early 1960s. Argues that union leadership effectively responded to teacher dissatisfaction with a militant action program by winning substantial benefits for the membership, but without advancing the professional status of teachers.

27. Counts, George S. *Dare the School Build a New Social Order?* New York: John Day, 1932. 56 pp. Reprint ed., New York: Arno Press, 1969. 56 pp.

A famous essay on ideals for American education which, although without mentioning the AFT, clearly influenced union programs of the thirties and forties.

28. _____. *School and Society in Chicago.* New York: Harcourt, Brace, 1928. 367 pp.

Two chapters concentrate on the fortunes of the CTF, 1893–1926, with special consideration given to the Loeb rule.

29. Cremin, Lawrence A. *The Transformation of the School: Progressivism in American Education, 1876–1957.* New York: Alfred A. Knopf, 1961. 387 pp.

A study of the Progressive Education Movement. Several AFT leaders, e.g., Dewey and Counts, were among its guiding lights. Cremin credits the AFT with great effectiveness in the defense of academic freedom and the campaign for adequate tenure laws.

30. Curoe, Philip R. V. *Educational Attitudes and Policies of Organized Labor in the United States.* New York: Bureau of Publications, Teachers College, Columbia University, 1929. 201 pp. Reprint ed., New York: Arno Press, 1969. 201 pp.

Contains a short section on the organizational philosophy of the early AFT and on the education programs of the AFL.

31. Dewey, John. *Education Today.* New York: G. P. Putnam's Sons, 1940. 373 pp.

In the chapter entitled "The Teacher and the Public," Dewey urges teachers to "ally themselves with their friends against their common foe, the privileged class, and in the alliance develop the character, skill and the intelligence that are necessary to make a democratic social order a fact."

32. Dodge, Chester C. *Reminiscences of a School Master.* Chicago: Ralph Fletcher Seymour, 1941. 141 pp.

The CTF and the Loeb rule controversy figure briefly in this autobiography.

33. Doherty, Robert E., ed. *Employer-Employee Relations in the Public Schools.* Ithaca, New York: New York State School of Industrial and Labor Relations, Cornell University, 1967. 145 pp.

Contains "Aspirations of the Empire State Federation of Teachers," a speech given by Albert Shanker at a conference held July, 1966.

34. Doherty, Robert E. and Walter E. Oberer. *Teachers, School Boards, and Collective Bargaining: A Changing of the Guard.* Ithaca, New York: New York State School of Industrial and Labor Relations, Cornell University, 1967. 139 pp.

Provides a brief review of AFT positions regarding collective bargaining and labor affiliation. An appendix compares sample AFT and NEA contracts.

35. Duryea, E. E. and Robert Fisk. *Faculty Unions and Collective Bargaining.* San Francisco: Jossey-Bass, 1973. 236 pp.

Characterizes the AFT as the most willing of all groups to take "a forthright adversary position in their bargaining relationships."

36. Elam, Stanley M., et al. *Readings on Collective Negotiations in Public Education.* Chicago: Rand McNally, 1967. 470 pp.

Of particular note are selections by Charles Cogen on

collective bargaining, Michael H. Moskow on the AFT–NEA rivalry, and Dick Dashiell on AFT victories in Detroit and Cleveland.

37. Elsbree, Willard S. *The American Teacher: Evolution of a Profession in a Democracy.* New York: American Book, 1939. 566 pp.

A short passage on the AFT predicts that the union will remain of minor significance in American education.

38. Fantini, Mario and Marilyn R. Gittell. *Decentralization: Achieving Reform.* New York: Praeger, 1973. 170 pp.

Offers a brief review of the UFT position on decentralization in the early 1970s.

39. Galenson, Walter. *The CIO Challenge to the AFL: A History of the American Labor Movement, 1935–1941.* Cambridge, Massachusetts: Harvard University Press, 1960. 732 pp.

Background reading on the CIO debate within the AFT.

40. Gittell, Marilyn R. *School Boards and School Policy: An Evaluation of Decentralization in New York City.* New York: Praeger, 1973. 169 pp.

Contrasts UFT positions before and after the establishment of community school boards.

41. Gittell, Marilyn R. and T. Edward Hollander. *Six Urban School Districts: A Comparative Study of Institutional Response.* New York: Praeger, 1968. 329 pp.

Contains information on locals in Chicago, Detroit, St. Louis, Baltimore, New York, and Philadelphia.

42. Hansen, Carl F. *Danger in Washington: The Story of My Twenty Years in the Public Schools in the Nation's Capital.* West Nyack, New York: Parker Publishing, 1968. 237 pp.

A former superintendent's memoirs. Discusses his opposition to the union over various issues.

43. Henry, Alice. *Women and the Labor Movement.* New York: George H. Doran, 1923. 232 pp. Reprint ed., New York: Arno Press, 1971. 241 pp.

The author, an AFT member, uses AFT history to illustrate the social achievements of American women.

44. Hentoff, Nat. *Peace Agitator: The Story of A. J. Muste.* New York: Macmillan, 1963. 269 pp.

    A biography of the director of Brookwood Labor College and renowned pacifist thinker who in the twenties was also an AFT vice president.

45. Iverson, Robert W. *The Communists and the Schools.* New York: Harcourt, Brace, 1959. 423 pp.

    Gives substantial coverage to action by the AFT leadership to expel individuals and locals because of membership in the Communist party.

46. Kirkendall, Lester A., et al. *Goals for American Education.* Chicago: American Federation of Teachers, 1948. 130 pp.

    The major union statement on the problems of American schools and educational goals following World War II.

47. Koch, Raymond and Charlotte Koch. *Educational Commune: The Story of Commonwealth College.* New York: Schocken Books, 1972. 211 pp.

    Commonwealth College was a resident workers' school in Mena, Arkansas, with the faculty composed of AFT, Local 194. The authors were students and staff members from 1925 until the demise of the institution in 1940.

48. La Noue, George R. and Bruce L. R. Smith. *The Politics of School Decentralization.* Lexington, Massachusetts: D. C. Heath, Lexington Books, 1973. 284 pp.

    Discusses the policies of local federations in Los Angeles, Washington, D.C., Detroit, and New York concerning decentralization plans.

49. Lieberman, Myron. *Education as a Profession.* Englewood Cliffs, New Jersey: Prentice-Hall, 1956. 540 pp.

    Includes chapters on collective bargaining and other issues before the AFT in the 1950s.

50. _____. *The Future of Public Education.* Chicago: The University of Chicago Press, 1960. 294 pp.

Argues that the AFT should tone down the fact of their labor affiliation in an effort to merge with the NEA.

51. Lieberman, Myron and Michael H. Moskow. *Collective Negotiations for Teachers: An Approach to School Administration.* Chicago: Rand McNally, 1966. 745 pp.
A major study on collective bargaining, covering the historical and legal background of the process, i.e., representation, selection of negotiating units, negotiating procedure, strikes, arbitration, and contracts. Each section of the book gives consideration to the AFT position by citing numerous cases.

52. Lutz, Frank W. and Joseph H. Azzarelli, eds. *Struggle for Power in Education.* New York: The Center for Applied Resources, 1966. 120 pp.
Includes a statement by David Selden defining teacher power.

53. Masters, Nicholas A., et al. *State Politics and the Public Schools: An Exploratory Analysis.* New York: Alfred A. Knopf, 1964. 319 pp.
Contains short segments on state federations in Illinois and Michigan.

54. Mayer, Martin. *The Teachers Strike: New York, 1968.* New York: Harper and Row, 1969. 122 pp.
A New York school official states that "the New York teachers' strike of 1968 seems to me the worst disaster my native city has experienced in my lifetime," but his book is not unsympathetic to the position of the UFT.

55. Melby, Ernest O., ed. *Mobilizing Educational Resources for Winning the War and the Peace.* Sixth Yearbook of the John Dewey Society. New York: Harper and Brothers, 1943. 242 pp.
The views expressed in this essay collection, especially in the contributions of George S. Counts and Theodore Brameld, parallel those of the AFT's Commission on Educational Reconstruction.

56. Miller, Roland M. *Prelude to Negotiations? Conflicts, Roles*

and Conditions, as Seen in Case Studies of Two New England School Systems. Cambridge, Massachusetts: The New England School Development Council, 1965. 58 pp.

Presents case studies involving locals in Meriden and Wethersfield, Connecticut.

57. Morris, James O. *Conflict Within the AFL: A Study of Craft versus Industrial Unionism, 1901–1938.* Ithaca, New York: Cornell University, 1958. 319 pp.

Contains significant material on Brookwood Labor College, particularly the withdrawal of AFL support in 1929. Morris contends that conflict between the college faculty and conservative unionists was inevitable.

58. Moskow, Michael H. *Teachers and Unions: The Applicability of Collective Bargaining to Public Education.* Philadelphia: University of Pennsylvania, Wharton School of Finance and Commerce, Industrial Research Unit, 1966. 288 pp.

Includes discussion of AFT policy on bargaining units, recognition, membership restrictions, and contracts.

59. Newell, Barbara W. *Chicago and the Labor Movement: Metropolitan Unionism in the 1930's.* Urbana, Illinois: University of Illinois Press, 1961. 288 pp.

A short section on the struggles of the CTU during the Depression.

60. Perry, Charles R. and Wesley A. Wildman. *The Impact of Negotiations in Public Education: The Evidence from the Schools.* Worthington, Ohio: Charles A. Jones, 1970. 254 pp.

Devotes a chapter to the "new militancy" of the AFT and the NEA.

61. Philley, Flora A. *Teacher, Help Yourself.* Chicago: The American Federation of Teachers, 1948. 157 pp.

A history of Gary (Indiana) Teachers Union, Local 4, which was a charter local of the AFT.

62. Rogers, David. *110 Livingston Street: Politics and Bureaucracy in the New York City Schools.* New York: Random House, 1968. 584 pp.

25

A study of desegregation problems in New York City schools. Written before the Ocean Hill-Brownsville dispute, the book credits the UFT with a decent civil rights record, but predicts increased tension with the black community.

63. Rosenthal, Alan. *Pedagogues and Power: Teacher Groups in School Politics.* Syracuse, New York: Syracuse University Press, 1969. 192 pp.

    Reviews AFT philosophy, the relative militancy of individual locals, and the successes in recent local elections. Particular attention is given to the UFT.

64. Shils, Edward B. and C. Taylor Whittler. *Teachers, Administrators, and Collective Bargaining.* New York: Thomas Y. Crowell Company, 1968. 580 pp.

    A survey comparing the AFT and NEA on local and state levels regarding organizational rivalry, militancy, and reactions to individual state laws and trends in school administration.

65. Sinclair, Upton. *The Goslings: A Study of the American Schools.* Pasadena, California: Upton Sinclair, 1924. 454 pp.

    A muckraker's guide to corruption in American schools, containing two chapters on AFT locals, plus isolated references to the union.

66. Smith, Robert, *et al. By Any Means Necessary.* San Francisco: Jossey-Bass, 1970. 370 pp.

    On Local 1352's strike at San Francisco State College in 1968–1969. The strike involved far more than AFT support for just the black and "Third World" student demands as headlined by the press. Genuine discontent among instructors regarding salaries and teaching conditions also caused the local to strike.

67. Smith, William Allen. *Indiana Public Schools: Unionism and Collective Negotiations.* Bloomington, Indiana: Indiana University School of Business, Division of Research, Business Information Bulletin 60, 1971. 142 pp.

    This study of collective bargaining by both AFT and NEA affiliates finds that it has obtained substantial gains for Indiana teachers in salaries and working conditions. The author hesitates, however, to predict the future effectiveness of collective bargaining.

68. Spero, Sterling D. *Government as Employer.* New York: Remsen Press, 1948. 503 pp. Reprint ed., Carbondale, Illinois: Southern Illinois University Press, 1972. 497 pp.

Discusses the early effect of the AFT on the NEA, the survival of the Chicago locals in the Depression of the thirties, and events leading to the expulsion of Local 5 in 1941.

69. Stinnett, Timothy M. *Turmoil in Teaching: A History of the Organizational Struggle for America's Teachers.* New York: Macmillan, 1968. 406 pp.

An NEA official discusses the AFT in relation to the events since 1962. He argues for "professionalism" and "integrity," and against labor affiliation.

70. Sturmthal, Adolf, ed. *White Collar Trade-Unions: Contemporary Developments in Industrial Societies.* Urbana, Illinois: University of Illinois Press, 1967. 412 pp.

Briefly summarizes AFT history in the context of worldwide union development.

71. Tice, Terrence N., ed. *Faculty Bargaining in the Seventies.* Ann Arbor, Michigan: The Institute of Continuing Legal Education, 1973. 408 pp.

Description and analysis of the process of collective bargaining in the academic sector.

72. Tice, Terrence N. and Grace W. Holmes. *Faculty Power: Collective Bargaining on Campus.* Ann Arbor, Michigan: The Institute of Continuing Legal Education, 1972. 368 pp.

Contains frequent references to AFT locals in the section "Faculty Organization" and in the appendices.

73. Urofsky, Melvin. *Why Teachers Strike: Teachers' Rights and Community Control.* Garden City, New York: Doubleday, Anchor Books, 1970. 349 pp.

Contains transcripts of interviews with twelve men who played major roles in the UFT strike of 1968. Included are Albert Shanker and Harold G. Israelson.

74. Wasserman, Miriam. *The School Fix, NYC, USA.* New York: Outerbridge and Dienstfrey, 1970. 568 pp.

    A long chapter on the UFT credits Albert Shanker and others with many years of progressive union leadership, but deplores the impasse of 1968 and the failure to achieve major school reform in New York.

75. Wattenberg, William W. *On the Educational Front: The Reactions of Teachers Associations in New York and Chicago.* New York: Columbia University Press, 1936. 218 pp.

    This "study in social psychology" states that the union functions as both a political pressure and a mass pressure organization. Includes discussion of the Chicago teachers' "revolt" of 1933 and the disputes within the AFT membership over the CIO and the Communist party.

76. Whitfield, Stephen J. *Scott Nearing: Apostle of American Radicalism.* New York: Columbia University Press, 1974. 269 pp.

    Briefly discusses Nearing's support for a leftist faction which challenged Linville and Lefkowitz for the leadership of Local 5.

II. ARTICLES

77. "Against Short Tenure for Teachers." *Survey*, 36 (July 8, 1916), 384.
    The CTF protests one-year contracts.

78. "The American Federation of Teachers." *Elementary School Journal*, 20 (October, 1919), 89–92.
    An editorial recognizes the need for a strong teacher federation, but regrets the union affiliation.

79. "An Appeal for a Teacher's Union." *American Teacher*, 5 (February, 1916), 24.
    Insists that "a teacher's plain duty is to organize."

80. "The Associated Teachers' Union of New York City." *School and Society*, 9 (May 17, 1919), 592–593.
    Describes the founding in 1919 of the University of New York faculty, Local 71.

81. "A Call to Organize." *American Teacher*, 2 (February, 1913), 27–28.
    Announces a meeting called by John Dewey and others to discuss the formation of a new organization which would speak for teacher interests.

82. Chenery, William L. "Adulterated Education." *New Republic*, 4 (October 23, 1915), 304–306.
    Fears the Loeb rule may erase the early victories of the CTF.

83. _____. "Catherine Goggin." *Life and Labor*, 6 (February, 1916), 23.
    A portrait of the CTF leader.

84. "The Chicago Board of Education and the Teachers' Federation." *School and Society*, 2 (October 16, 1915), 565–568; and (October 30, 1915), 636–639.
    Quotation and discussion of the Loeb rule in defense of the CTF.

85. "The Chicago Decision." *American Teacher*, 6 (May, 1917), 72 and 77.
    The AFT deplores a court decision enforcing the Loeb rule.

86. "Chicago Schools and Politics." *Elementary School Journal*, 16 (October, 1915), 54–57.
    Concerns the passage of the Loeb rule, quoting an editorial sympathetic to the CTF.

87. "The Chicago Situation." *Elementary School Journal*, 17 (September, 1916), 3–5.
    Discusses the Loeb rule and advocates a strict application of the merit system.

88. "The Chicago Teachers and Public Welfare." *American Teacher*, 4 (November, 1915), 133–135; "A Critical Situation," *American Teacher*, 4 (September, 1915), 107–108.
    Discusses the fight by the CTF for fair tax evaluation and the efforts of the Chicago Board of Education to prohibit CTF affiliation with the AFT.

89. "The Chicago Teachers' Federation and 'Life and Labor.'" *Life and Labor*, 3 (May, 1913), 146–147.
    The CTF recommends to its members *Life and Labor* for current information on reform legislation.

90. "The Chicago Teachers' Federation and the Board of Education." *School and Society*, 5 (May 5, 1917), 526–527.
    A report on the Illinois Supreme Court decision upholding the Loeb rule.

91. "Chicago's Franchise Taxes—and New York's." *American Monthly Review of Reviews*, 24 (December, 1901), 656–657.
    A brief report on the CTF tax victory of 1901.

92. "Chicago's Unionized Teachers." *Literary Digest*, 51 (October 2, 1915), 700.
    A report on the conflicting views of the CTF as held by the Chicago press.

93. Cook, William A. "Rise and Significance of the American

Federation of Teachers." *Elementary School Journal*, 21 (February, 1921), 444–460.
Views union affiliation as "dangerous" but praises the reform efforts of the AFT.

94. "The Crisis." *American Teacher*, 5 (April, 1916), 55–56.
The New York Teachers' League (forerunner of Local 5) *vs.* the New York City Board of Education over the issue of labor affiliation.

95. "Democracy in Education." *Public*, 9 (May 5, 1906), 100–103.
On the CTF fight against "despotic tendencies," i.e., big business domination of the Chicago schools.

96. Dewey, John. "The Bearings of Pragmatism upon Education." *Progressive Journal of Education*, 1 (December, 1908), 1-3; (January, 1909), 5–8; (February, 1909), 6–7.
A basic exposition of Dewey's educational philosophy. The *Journal* was a forerunner of the *American Teacher,* and Dewey was a consistent advocate of teachers' unions and a frequent contributor to the *American Teacher.*

97. _____. "Democracy in Education." *Elementary School Teacher*, 4 (December, 1903), 193–204.
A formulation of AFT philosophy.

98. _____. "Industrial Education and Democracy." *Survey*, 29 (March 22, 1913), 870–871. Reprint of "An Undemocratic Proposal" in the *American Teacher*, 2 (January, 1913), 2–4.
Advocates a well-administered vocational education program in public schools rather than a separate school system for vocational education under the direction of industrialists.

99. _____. "Professional Organization of Teachers." *American Teacher*, 5 (September, 1916), 99–101.
Dewey maintains that "every teacher should feel proud to be affiliated with the labor unions."

100. "The Dismissal of Chicago Teachers." *School Review*, 24 (September, 1916), 550–551.

This editorial blames the formulation of the Loeb rule on the "irritating" tactics of the CTF.

101. "The Dismissal of Chicago Teachers Belonging to the Teachers' Federation." *School and Society*, 4 (July 15, 1916), 93–94.
      A report naming and evaluating the competency of the dismissed teachers.

102. Dorr, Rheta Childe. "What's the Matter with the Public Schools?" Part 3, "The Robbery of the Schools." *Delineator*, 73 (January, 1909), 99–100+
      The CTF tax victory of 1901 is discussed as part of a general survey of school finance problems.

103. "Editorial Notes." *School Review*, 15 (February, 1907), 160–165.
      Chicago Superintendent Cooley *vs.* the CTF.

104. Engdahl, J. L. "Chicago Teachers' Federation." *American Teacher*, 4 (October, 1915), 118–119.
      Discusses a dispute between the CTF leadership and William Rainey Harper, president of the University of Chicago.

105. Frayne, Hugh. "Public School Teachers in Affiliation with the American Federation of Labor." *American Teacher*, 5 (February, 1916), 18–19.
      An AFL organizer in New York explains how teachers strengthen the reform movement through labor affiliation.

106. Frohlich, May T. "New Orleans Teachers Organize." *American Teacher*, 8 (April, 1919), 80–82.
      The organization of the Associate Teachers League of New Orleans, Local 36.

107. Fuller, Edward H. "Educational Associations and Organizations in the United States." *Educational Review*, 55 (April, 1918), 300–325.
      Contains two pages of information on the National Federation of Teachers and the CTF.

108. Fursman, Ida L. M. "Freedom, Ignorance, and Poverty." *American Teacher*, 5 (October, 1916), 120–124.
The CTF president criticizes the financial priorities of the Chicago School Board.

109. Gilman, Charlotte Perkins. "Education and Social Progress." *American Teacher*, 1 (December, 1912), 134–135.
In view of their vital service to society, teachers deserve better salaries and more professional recognition.

110. Glassberg, Benjamin. "The Organization of Teachers in the United States." *Dial*, 67 (September 20, 1919), 242–244.
A brief survey of teacher federations, 1899–1919.

111. Goggin, Catherine. "Inaugural Address." *Chicago Teacher and School Board Journal*, 1 (June, 1899), 307–310.
A presidential address, reviewing the reasons for the founding of the CTF two years earlier.

112. Gompers, Samuel. "The American School and the Working Man." In *Addresses and Proceedings of the National Education Association*, vol. 54, pp. 175–182. Ann Arbor: National Education Association, 1916. See also *School and Society*, 4 (July 22, 1916), 127–133.
An address before the NEA, urging labor affiliation for teachers.

113. "Greetings." *American Teacher*, 1 (January, 1912), 1.
The introductory editorial of the *American Teacher*, a magazine "devoted to . . . publishing information and discussions calculated to improve the professional and social status of the teachers and the work of schools."

114. Haley, Margaret A. "Why Teachers Should Organize." In *Addresses and Proceedings of the National Education Association*, 1904, pp. 145–152. Winona, Minnesota: National Education Association, 1904.
Haley, business agent for the CTF, views education as caught up in a struggle between two contradictory ideals, the democratic *vs.* the "industrial" way of life.

115. Hall, G. Stanley. "Certain Degenerative Tendencies Among Teachers." *Pedagogical Seminary*, 12 (December, 1905), 454–463.
Support for the contention that teacher unionism is a "vice."

116. Hard, William. "Chicago's Five Maiden Aunts." *American Magazine*, 62 (September, 1906), 481–489.
Credit for much of the success of the Chicago reform movement goes to unionists Margaret Haley and Mary McDowell, reformer Jane Addams, and other women activists.

117. _____. "Margaret Haley, Rebel." *The Times Magazine*, 1 (January, 1907), 231–237. See also "The Fight for the Schools," *The Times Magazine* (February, 1907), 363–368.
Lauds Haley and the elementary school teachers for their successful fight against big-business domination of public education in Chicago.

118. "In Re the Loeb Rule." *Chamberlin's*, 14 (May, 1916), 24–25.
Presents the CTF's right to labor affiliation.

119. "An International Union of Teachers." *American Teacher*, 5 (May, 1916), 69–70.
An announcement on the founding of the AFT.

120. Jackman, Wilbur S. "Teachers' Federation and Labor-Unionism." *Elementary School Teacher*, 5 (March, 1905), 439–446.
An editorial supporting the CTF, states that the union represents "the true interest of the whole people."

121. Kelley, Florence, et al. "A Symposium on Teachers' Unions." *American Teacher*, 8 (February, 1919), 51–43+; (March, 1919), 59–61.
A compendium of arguments for and against labor affiliation.

122. Kennedy, John C. "Labor Unions and the Schools." *American Teacher*, 4 (October, 1915), 116–117.
A Chicago alderman encourages labor affiliation.

123. Kimball, Hattie. "Federation of Teachers." *Journal of Education*, 90 (September 11, 1919), 231.
   A defense of labor affiliation as "a stand for real democracy."

124. Lampson, L. V. "The Smith–Towner Bill Revised." *American Teacher*, 8 (September, 1919), 155–157. See also "The Education Bill," *American Teacher*, 8 (June, 1919), 135.
   AFT endorsement of a federal Department of Education.

125. Lefkowitz, Abraham. "The Teachers Union: Past and Future." *American Teacher*, 6 (June, 1917), 86–87+.
   An early review of Local 5 progress.

126. "Letting in the Professor." *Survey*, 42 (May 24, 1919), 314.
   A brief report on early college locals.

127. Linville, Henry R. "Plans for the Development of the Teachers Union." *American Teacher*, 8 (April, 1919), 93–95.
   Advocates the creation of salaried union offices.

128. Loeb, Jacob M. "The Business Man and the Public Service." In *Addresses and Proceedings of the National Education Association*, vol. 54, pp. 351–355, 356–359. Ann Arbor: National Education Association, 1916.
   Chicago School Board President Loeb denounces the Chicago Federation of Labor. Ella Flagg Young, Chicago Superintendent of Schools, defends labor's involvement in education.

129. Loeb, Max. "The Radical Movement in Education." *Survey*, 37 (December 9, 1916), 272–273.
   An endorsement of labor affiliation for educators as "a movement toward truer democracy."

130. _____. "The Teacher and the Union." *American Teacher*, 6 (February, 1917), 18–22.
   Encourages union membership for teachers.

131. Lovett, John L. "Fighting for Chicago Public Schools." *Chamberlin's*, 15 (June, 1917), 11–13.
   Schools have benefited from union victories.

132. "Loyalty and Unionism." *American Teacher*, 7 (May–June, 1918), 99.
   Labor unions uphold the goals fought for in the World War.

133. McAndrew, William. "The Control of the Teacher's Job." *American Teacher*, 5 (September, 1916), 103–105.
   A New York school administrator congratulates the CTF.

134. McCoy, W. T. "What We Have Accomplished." *American Teacher*, 8 (June, 1919), 134–135.
   A review of the victories of the Chicago teachers' locals.

135. "The Maid of Chicago." *Journal of Education*, 54 (August 15, 1901), 1–2.
   A discussion of the CTF tax victory, praises Margaret Haley and Catherine Goggin for their work.

136. "Milk Drivers and Professors." *Literary Digest*, 62 (July 19, 1919), 25.
   A CTF report claiming that milk drivers, plumbers, and janitors are paid more than teachers.

137. Miller, Frederick. "Teachers' Unions at Work." *American Teacher*, 5 (February, 1916), 19–23.
   Praise for the program of the CTF and the English National Union of Teachers.

138. _____. "What a Teachers' Union Is Not." *American Teacher*, 5 (April, 1916), 61–62.
   Unionized teachers can not be called out on sympathy strikes.

139. "Miss Margaret A. Haley." *Current Literature*, 36 (June, 1904), 612–613.
   A portrait of the CTF leader.

140. Morrison, Benjamin. "The Cleveland School Board and the Teachers Union." *American Teacher*, 3 (September, 1914), 98–101. See also "On the Rights of Teachers to Demand Their Rights," *American Teacher*, 3 (December, 1914), 156–157.
   An account of the school board firing of the teachers who

attempted to form a union and affiliate with the Cleveland Federation of Labor.

141. Mortimer, Florence C. "The Value of Labor Unions." *American Teacher*, 8 (December, 1919), 220–225.
Analyzes the value of organized labor's support for education and teachers' unions.

142. Myers, C. E. "Should Teachers' Organizations Affiliate with the American Federation of Labor?" *School and Society*, 10 (November 22, 1919), 594–597.
Presents the point of view that "unionized teachers are a threat to democracy."

143. Nearing, Scott. "The New Education." *American Teacher*, 5 (January, 1916), 2–6.
"A successful school . . . turns out children . . . well fitted to cope with the world in which they live."

144. O'Reilly, Mary. "What Organization of the Teachers Means to Labor." *Life and Labor*, 5 (November, 1915), 166–168.
Stresses the value of a united effort for reform legislation.

145. Persons, Warren M. "The Chicago Teachers Federation." *Commons*, 10 (August, 1905), 441–445.
Praises the CTF for the tax assessment victories and for labor affiliation.

146. "The Proposed Union of Cleveland Teachers." *Survey*, 32 (August 8, 1914), 477–478.
A report of the success of the Cleveland school board in its effort to block labor affiliation for teachers.

147. "A Radical Departure in Unionism." *Scribner's Magazine*, 33 (June, 1903), 763–764.
Criticizes the affiliation of the CTF with the Chicago Federation of Labor.

148. Ramsay, Charles Cornell. "Impressions of the NEA Convention for 1903." *Education*, 24 (September, 1903), 44–49.

Delegates express disapproval of the CTF and the views of John Dewey and Margaret Haley.

149. Rankin, Jeanette. "Unionism among Teachers." *American Teacher*, 7 (May-June, 1918), 107-108.
Expresses the opinion that unions are essential to democracy.

150. Ricker, David Swing. "The School Teacher Unionized." *Educational Review*, 30 (November, 1905), 344-374.
Concerned that membership in the CTF might taint the educator with the corruption of ward politics.

151. _____. "Unionizing the School Teachers." *World To-Day*, 8 (April, 1905), 394-402.
A discussion of the founding of the CTF, affiliation with the AFL, and plans for the National Federation of Teachers.

152. "The Rights of Teachers." *New Republic*, 19 (May 10, 1919), 36-37.
A favorable report on AFT growth.

153. Rood, Florence. "A New Type of City School Administration." *American Teacher*, 3 (June, 1914), 88.
Suggests that local federations advise school boards on educational policy.

154. "Roster of Locals of the AFT." *American Teacher*, 8 (March, 1919), 69-71. Continued in *American Teacher*, 8 (June, 1919), 142; 8 (October, 1919), 190.
Cites the locations of Locals 2 through 112.

155. Ruediger, W. C. "Unionism among Teachers." *School and Society*, 8 (November 16, 1918), 589-591. Reply by Alfred H. Foreman, *School and Society*, 8 (December 7, 1918), 682-684.
Early arguments regarding labor affiliation.

156. Schmalhausen, Sam. "The Value of the Teachers' Union." *American Teacher*, 6 (November, 1917), 132-134.
An increase in the size of the union is necessary in order to make collective bargaining successful.

157. "A School Childrens' Strike." *Commons*, 10 (June, 1905), 329–330.
    Rejects charges that the CTF has encouraged truancy.

158. "The School Question in Chicago." *Elementary School Teacher*, 7 (February, 1907), 361–367.
    An editor claims that only union organization affords teachers a professional voice.

159. "School Teachers and the Right to Organize." *Life and Labor*, 5 (September, 1915), 145–146.
    Encourages AFL-affiliated teacher federations.

160. "Shall School Teachers Join Labor Unions?" *Survey*, 35 (October 2, 1915), 1–2.
    The CTF defies the Chicago School Board on the question of labor affiliation.

161. Snedden, David. "The Professional Improvement of Teachers and Teaching through Organization." *School and Society*, 10 (November 8, 1919), 531–539.
    Favors independent organization but not union affiliation.

162. Snodgrass, Margaret. "The American Federation of Teachers." *American Federationist*, 23 (September, 1916), 788–790.
    Describes the first three months of the AFT in Chicago.

163. Stair, Bird. "The Unionizing of Teachers." *School and Society*, 10 (December 13, 1919), 699–703.
    Only labor affiliation for teachers will promote professional spirit and reform without endangering the public interests.

164. Stecker, Freeland G. "Report of the Financial Secretary of the American Federation of Teachers." *American Teacher*, 7 (September, 1918), 148–150.
    On the chartering of nineteen new locals.

165. Stillman, Charles B. "Educational Recommendations of the Atlantic City Convention of the American Federation of Labor." *American Teacher*, 8 (September, 1919), 3–5.

Resolutions on federal aid to education, freedom of teachers to join unions.

166. _____. "Four Months of Progress." *American Teacher*, 8 (January, 1919), 12–18.
News of new locals and committee reports.

167. _____. "Report of the President of the American Federation of Teachers." *American Teacher*, 7 (September, 1918), 140–148.
A review of early union problems and successes.

168. _____. "Teachers and Organized Labor." *American Federationist*, 26 (September, 1919), 812–813. See also *Federal Employee*, 4 (December 13, 1919), 732–733.
By better preparing students for democracy, AFT members repay the labor movement for its support.

169. _____. "Tenure of Position of Superintendents and Teachers." *American Teacher*, 6 (March, 1917), 34–37.
Tenure for both the school superintendent and the teacher is necessary for academic freedom.

170. _____. "The Union Movement Among Teachers." *Life and Labor*, 9 (November, 1919), 277–280. See also *American Teacher*, 5 (September, 1916), 101–103.
From an address before a union teachers' caucus at the 1916 NEA convention defending labor affiliation.

171. _____. "The Washburn College Situation." *American Teacher*, 8 (October, 1919), 182–183.
Discusses the dismissal of a college teacher in Kansas because of his union membership.

172. Stillman, Charles B. and C. C. Willard. "The Teachers' Outlook." *Public*, 21 (March, 1918), 372–373.
On AFT support for the war effort.

173. "The Taxation of Franchises." *World's Work*, 3 (December, 1901), 1474–1475.
The Illinois Supreme Court supports the CTF case for a tax reassessment of utility companies.

174. "A Tax-Reform Victory." *Outlook*, 69 (November 2, 1901), 527–528.
The tax-assessment victory of the CTF.

175. "Teachers! Freedom Through Organization." *American Federationist*, 23 (June, 1916), 476–478.
Describes the founding of the AFT and shows the Loeb rule to be a threat to its continued existence.

176. "Teachers' Right to Organize." *American Federationist*, 22 (October, 1915), 857–860.
Support for the fight against the Loeb rule.

177. "Teachers' Right to Organize Affirmed." *American Federationist*, 21 (December, 1914), 1083–1085.
A Cleveland court supports the teachers' right to affiliate with organized labor.

178. "Teachers' Service and Rights." *American Federationist*, 22 (November, 1915), 981–982.
Reports a court injunction striking down the Loeb rule.

179. "Teachers, Their Duties and Ours." *American Federationist*, 21 (July, 1914), 562–564.
Support given to teachers by the Cleveland Federation of Labor.

180. "Teachers' Unions in Chicago." *School Review*, 23 (October, 1915), 559–560.
Militant unionism is called "intolerable."

181. Turner, Victoria B. "American Federation of Teachers." *Monthly Labor Review*, 9 (August, 1919), 247–255.
Information on early AFT history, including names of the first officers and an evaluation of the union's programs.

182. "Unionism Among the Teachers of the Capital City." *American Teacher*, 7 (April, 1918), 95.
Stresses the pro-union sentiment of some of the Washington, D.C., newspapers. Reviews the state of teacher unionism in the city.

183. "Unionized Teachers." *School and Society*, 2 (September 18, 1915), 419–420.
    Reports the views of Margaret Haley and Samuel Gompers on education.

184. Wellers, Meta. "The Birth of Teachers' Organizations." *Journal of Education*, 84 (November 2, 1916), 440.
    A humorous note on the founding of the CTF.

185. _____. "The Black Year." *Journal of Education*, 51 (May 24, 1900), 329.
    A brief report on the CTF reaction to salary cuts.

186. "What Teachers' Unions Have Done and Can Do." *American Teacher*, 5 (May, 1916), 70–71.
    The first program of Local 5.

187. "What Teachers Want." *School and Society*, 10 (July 19, 1919), 81–83.
    Discussion of an early phase of the AFT–NEA rivalry.

188. "Which Sort of Union?" *School and Society*, 10 (October 25, 1919), 494–495.
    The early Local 5.

189. "Why Chicago's Teachers Unionized." *Harper's Weekly*, 60 (June 19, 1915), 598–599.
    Credits the CTF with producing "a school system so much better than the old that comparison fails."

190. Winship, A. E. "Twenty-Five Years of Chicago." *Journal of Education*, 71 (June 16, 1910), 685–689.
    A survey of important events, including the founding of the CTF.

1920–1929

191. "An Adequate Teachers' Pension Is Basic Need." *American Federation of Teachers Monthly Bulletin*, 5 (January, 1926), 1+.

Concluded in *American Federation of Teachers Monthly Bulletin*, 5 (February, 1926), 3.
Outlines essential features of a good pension plan and reviews what was then offered in major cities.

192. Adler, Felix. "Shall Teachers Affiliate with Labor Unions?" *Standard*, 6 (March, 1920), 224–232.
Believes that union membership conflicts with the duty to serve all the people.

193. "The American Federation of Teachers." *Elementary School Journal*, 21 (March, 1921), 481–483.
Opposition to the AFT proposal for a greater teacher voice in school affairs.

194. Ameringer, Oscar. See entry 209.

195. Barker, Mary C. "Address of the President." *American Teacher*, 12 (September, 1927), 3–5.
Discusses responsibilities of teachers.

196. _____. "The Atlanta Public School Teachers Association." *American Teacher*, 12 (March, 1928), 4–6.
A brief history of the Atlanta local founded in 1905 and affiliated with the AFT in 1920.

197. _____. "Federation of Teachers Issues Program of Action." *American Federation of Teachers Monthly Bulletin*, 5 (September, 1925), 1+.
A presidential address equates union membership with professional consciousness.

198. _____. "President's Address." *American Teacher*, 11 (September, 1926), 3–5.
Concentrates on various organizational problems.

199. _____. "President's Address to the Thirteenth Convention of the American Federation of Teachers." *American Teacher*, 14 (October, 1929), 1–3.
Remarks focus on local organizing techniques.

200. Barron, James P. "Campaign of Local 89 for Adequate

Support of Atlanta's Public Schools." *American Teacher,* 12 (March, 1928), 12–14.

Local president writes of a successful campaign for a tax increase.

201. "The Better School Service." *American Federation of Teachers Semi-Monthly Bulletin,* 1 (February 20, 1922), 1.

On AFT help for local campaigns toward better salaries and work standards.

202. Blake, Katherine Devereaux. "Why I Am a Member of the Teachers Union." *American Teacher,* 13 (November, 1928), 3–5.

A retired principal's views.

203. Brewer, John M. "The Question of Unions in the Teachers' Profession." *School and Society,* 15 (January 14, 1922), 41–45. See also *American Federation of Teachers Semi-Monthly Bulletin,* 1 (February 5, 1922), 1+.

Harvard Professor Brewer provides answers to standard objections to labor affiliation.

204. "Brookwood Asks Hearing on A.F. of L. Charges." *American Teacher,* 13 (September, 1928), 8.

Numerous union leaders protest the AFL Executive Council attack on the labor college.

205. Byrnes, Mary, et al. "Teacher Tenure: Report of the Permanent Committee to the A.F.T. 1929 Convention." *American Teacher,* 14 (December, 1929), 20–23.

Presents arguments and evidence for use in state legislative tenure proposals.

206. Calverton, V. F. "Dr. Calhoun and Brookwood." *New Republic,* 59 (August 7, 1929), 314–315. Comment by Calhoun, *New Republic,* 60 (August 21, 1929), 20. See also *New Republic,* 60 (October 9, 1929), 208.

Clay Fulks argues that the dismissal of faculty member Arthur W. Calhoun would never occur at Commonwealth College, Arkansas.

207. "Chicago Conference of the American Federation." *School and Society*, 11 (January 10, 1920), 47.
Convention resolutions calling for federal aid to education and separate locals for administrators were approved.

208. Clohesy, Agnes B. "Some Objectives of the Elementary Teachers Union." *American Teacher*, 12 (May, 1928), 19–20.
Chicago Local 199 adopts a twelve-point program.

209. Coaldigger, Adam. "What the American Federation of Teachers Is Doing and Attempting to Do." *American Teacher*, 14 (September, 1929), 12–13.
Writing under this nom de plume, Oscar Ameringer discusses the effect of a traditional European education, with its emphasis upon discipline and rote learning, upon his own youth.

210. Coffman, Lotus D. "Teachers' Associations." *M.S.T.A. Quarterly Review*, 2 (March, 1920), 13–19.
A prominent educator identifies NEA objections to the AFT. Reply by Henry R. Linville, "Teachers' Unions as Agencies in Social Progress," *M.S.T.A. Quarterly Review*, 2 (June, 1920), 6–7, 17–20.

211. "Collective Bargaining by Teachers." *School and Society*, 11 (May 8, 1920), 558–559.
A Cleveland Teachers Federation resolution favors collective bargaining and tenure.

212. "Convention Notes." *American Teacher*, 11 (October, 1926), 8–11.
Establishment of new committees on tenure, educational trends, professional improvement.

213. Cunningham, William. "Commonwealth College—An Educational Mutant." *World Tomorrow*, 12 (December, 1929), 503–505.
The program and ideals of Commonwealth College.

214. Curtis, Winterton C. "Unionization from the Standpoint of a University Teacher." *Educational Review*, 60 (September,

1920), 91–105. Negative view by Arthur O. Lovejoy, *Educational Review*, 60 (September, 1920), 60, 106–119.

A debate between two eminent scholars over the appropriateness of labor affiliation for university teachers.

215. Dent, Mary C. and Elizabeth Draper. "Union Activities in Washington, D.C. Since 1916." *American Teacher*, 13 (June, 1929), 22–24.

A brief history of Local 8.

216. Dewey, John. "Labor Politics and Labor Education." *New Republic*, 57 (January 9, 1929), 211–213. Condensed in *School and Society*, 29 (January 19, 1929), 92–93.

Dewey defends Brookwood Labor College against attacks by Matthew Woll and the AFL Executive Council.

217. _____. "Why I Am a Member of the Teachers Union." *American Teacher*, 12 (January, 1928), 3–6.

A famous defense of teachers' efforts to improve their economic and social status through labor affiliation.

218. Edmunds, Amy G. "Teachers' Tenure in Minneapolis." *American Teacher*, 11 (March, 1927), 6–7.

Minnesota Federation of Teachers wins tenure protection for Minneapolis teachers.

219. Everett, R. W. "Report of the Committee on Academic Freedom and Tenure." *American Teacher*, 11 (March, 1927), 3–5+.

A review of state tenure laws.

220. Flexner, Jean Atherton. "Brookwood." *New Republic*, 43 (August 5, 1925), 287–289.

An introduction to the philosophy of the labor college.

221. Frank, Glenn. "Should Teachers Unionize?" *Century Magazine*, 101 (February, 1921), 529–532. See also *American Teacher*, 9 (February, 1921), 36–37.

Favors AFT membership provided the union recognizes a commitment to industrial democracy and strikes if necessary.

222. "Freedom to Teach the Truth Must Not Be Crushed." *American Federation of Teachers Monthly Bulletin*, 5 (March, 1926), 1+.

Historic AFT convention resolutions on academic freedom.

223. Gaines, I. J. "How and Why the Chatham County Teachers Affiliated." *American Teacher*, 13 (June, 1929), 3–4.

The organization of Savannah (Georgia) AFT, Local 207.

224. Gaines, W. W. "The Atlanta Public School Teachers Association and the Board of Education." *American Teacher*, 12 (March, 1928), 7–8.

The record of cooperation between Local 89 and the Atlanta School Board to provide quality education for Atlanta children.

225. Groves, Harold M. "On Being a 'Joiner.'" *American Teacher*, 11 (September, 1926), 8–10.

Reasons for college teacher membership in a labor union.

226. "A Half-Century of Workers' Education." *American Teacher*, 57 (December, 1927), 13–19.

A history of Local 189, containing articles by Staughton Lynd, Al Nash, et al.

227. Hanson, Florence Curtis. "The American Federation of Teachers and Strikes." *School and Society*, 25 (January 8, 1927), 52–53.

Reaffirmation of the AFT no-strike policy.

228. _____. "Should the American Federation of Teachers Be Supported?" *Nation's Schools*, 2 (December, 1928), 22–28. Dissenting views in "The School Executive Looks at the Teachers' Federation," *Nation's Schools*, 3 (March, 1929), 43–46.

A debate between the executive secretary of the AFT and a school executive over the role of organization in the achievement of teacher professionalization.

229. _____. "Teachers and the Power Trust." *Nation*, 127 (August 29, 1928), 202–203.

Expresses AFT opposition to dispensing corporate propaganda through the public schools.

230. Harris, J.K. "Framed." *Survey,* 55 (January 15, 1926), 469–470.
Discusses how Brookwood Labor College helps workers develop their full potential.

231. Hibbard, Walter H. "Courage and Co-Operation: Providence, R.I., Local 197." *American Teacher,* 13 (January, 1929), 19–20.
A summary of the past year's program.

232. Jacobs, Manuel Joseph. "A Comparison of the Philosophic Concept of the NEA and the American Federation of Teachers." *Sierra Educational News,* 25 (October, 1929), 18–21. See also *American Teacher,* 14 (October, 1929), 19–20.
Focuses upon the AFT freedom from administrative control.

233. Jones, Jerome. "The Relation of the Atlanta Public School Teachers Association to Organized Labor." *American Teacher,* 12 (March, 1928), 6–7.
A labor journalist affirms that the teachers are welcome "new blood" in the labor movement.

234. Kerchen, J. L. "Mutual Aid of American Federation of Teachers and Workers' Education." *American Teacher,* 11 (June, 1927), 11–12.
Regrets a lack of actual cooperation despite organizational affiliation.

235. "The Lancaster Opinion." *Educational Review,* 60 (September, 1920), 164–167.
In a Pennsylvania case, the first ruling by a state superintendent on teacher unionism supports the dismissal of teachers for participation in the labor movement.

236. "Launching Local No. 199." *American Teacher,* 12 (May, 1928), 16–18.
A new Chicago elementary teachers' local.

237. Lefkowitz, Abraham. "Affiliation with Labor." *American Teacher*, 12 (January, 1928), 10+.
A six-point defense of the AFT.

238. _____. "Impressions of the 13th Annual Convention of the A.F. of T." *American Teacher*, 14 (November, 1929), 12–14.
Finds a "new spirit" alive in the union.

239. _____. "The Lusk Laws." *American Federation of Teachers Semi-Monthly Bulletin*, 1 (December 20, 1921), 3.
A condemnation of repressive "Red Scare" legislation enacted in New York.

240. _____. "Shall Brookwood and Academic Freedom Die?" *American Teacher*, 13 (October, 1928), 25–26.
Demands a public hearing on AFL charges against Brookwood Labor College.

241. _____. "The Story of a Struggle for a Living Wage." *American Teacher*, 12 (November, 1927), 5–6.
Federation politics in New York since 1919.

242. Leonard, Louise. "Workers Education in the South." *American Teacher*, 13 (November, 1928), 8–10. See also *American Teacher*, 14 (December, 1929), 10–13.
A survey of the Southern Summer School for women industrial workers at Sweet Briar College in Virginia.

243. Linville, Henry R. "Program of Action of the Teachers' Union of New York City for the Year 1921-1922." *School and Society*, 14 (October 22, 1921), 343–344. See also *School and Society*, 14 (November 5, 1921), 404.
Calls for sabbatical leaves, reduction of class sizes, improved facilities.

244. _____. "The Teachers' Union Position on the Lusk Legislation." *American Federation of Teachers Semi-Monthly Bulletin*, 2 (November 20, 1922), 1+.
Charges that the Lusk laws forbid even democratic reform.

245. Little, Mary V. and Elizabeth E. Dix. "Present and Future

Objectives of Local No. 52." *American Teacher*, 12 (March, 1928), 18–20.

The Memphis local supports the sixteen goals of the 1925 AFT convention.

246. "Lusk School Laws Repealed." *American Federation of Teachers Semi-Monthly Bulletin*, 2 (May 5, 1923), 1.

Governor Alfred E. Smith signs the law repealing the Lusk laws.

247. Lyons, Marian C. "The Chicago Situation: Some Lost Spiritual Values." *American Teacher*, 11 (April, 1927), 5–7.

Opposition to board-imposed "efficiency" measures.

248. McCoy, William T. "Miss Weeks on Unionization." *American Federation of Teachers Semi-Monthly Bulletin*, 1 (November 5, 1921), 1+.

An articulate defense of the union contribution to professional integrity, written as a reply to an attack on the AFT published in the *Chicago Schools Journal*.

249. McLean, Samuel Gerald. "The California State Federation of the American Federation of Teachers." *American Teacher*, 11 (June, 1927), 3–4.

Cites major developments in California since 1920.

250. McMillen, P. A. "Campaign for Tenure in Minnesota." *American Teacher*, 11 (May, 1927), 3–4.

A state federation's effort to secure passage of a tenure law.

251. Mason, Mary L. and Eleanor Robinson. "Local 27 of the A.F. of T.: A Brief Summary of Its History, Achievements and Goals." *American Teacher*, 12 (March, 1928), 23–24.

A history of a black teachers' local in Washington, D. C.

252. Mickey, Louise D. "Selma Borchardt Honored by Teachers Union, Local No. 8." *American Teacher*, 12 (March, 1928), 21–22.

Recognition of the work of Selma Borchardt as AFT legislative representative.

253. Minard, Jeannette. "California Tenure Law." *American Teacher*, 12 (April, 1928), 4–5.
A defense of the 1921 and 1927 California tenure laws.

254. Mohr, Paul J. "Sabbatical Leave." *American Teacher*, 11 (June, 1927), 4.
California State Federation of Teachers is successful in its effort to win passage of a state law enabling local school boards to grant sabbatical leaves to public school teachers.

255. _____. "San Francisco Federation of Teachers No. 61." *American Teacher*, 13 (April, 1929), 4–5.
Tenth anniversary programs for Local 61.

256. Muste, A. J. "Labor Education and Summer Schooling." *Survey*, 54 (September 15, 1925), 633–635.
Two years of worker education summer schools at Brookwood Labor College.

257. Oakley, Genevieve. "Tenure in Memphis." *American Teacher*, 13 (June, 1929), 20–21.
Describes the long fight for a state tenure law.

258. O'Hanlon, John M. "Why Organized Labor Welcomes the Teachers." *American Teacher*, 13 (December, 1928), 12–15.
Cooperation in support for reform legislation in New York State.

259. O'Hare, Kate Richards. "Who Said Jurisdiction?" *American Teacher*, 13 (October, 1928), 17–18.
A spokesman for Commonwealth College defends labor education.

260. Overstreet, Harry A. "Organized Teachers and Organized Labor." *American Teacher*, 9 (March, 1920), 55–58.
Maintains teachers are not demeaned by labor affiliation.

261. Overstreet, Harry A. and David Snedden. "Should Teachers Affiliate With Organized Labor?" *Survey*, 43 (March 13, 1920), 736–737.
Overstreet says that the AFT promotes "industrial

53

democracy"; Snedden replies that the union infects schools with "partisanship."

262. Page, Myra. "Fascism in American Education." *American Teacher*, 14 (September, 1929), 19–20.
A radical view of the Seattle case.

263. Parsons, E. Duelly. "Americanization in Minneapolis." *American Teacher*, 9 (March, 1920), 53–54.
A union teacher is charged with un-American activity.

264. Pertinax. "Retrospect on No. 61." *American Teacher*, 12 (April, 1928), 12–13.
An account of San Francisco Local 61.

265. Pittman, Carlotta. "The Memphis Teachers Association Local 52." *American Teacher*, 12 (March, 1928), 16–18.
A brief history of Local 52.

266. _____. "Salary Increases in Memphis." *American Teacher*, 13 (October, 1928), 29.
A victory achieved with community support.

267. "Platform of Principles for the Class Room Teachers. Academic Freedom for Teachers and Pupils." *American Teacher*, 11 (September, 1926), 11–12; 11 (October, 1926), 17.
Formulated by the Chicago Federation of Women High School Teachers, Local 3.

268. Price, Richard R. "Should Teachers Unionize under the American Federation of Labor?" *School and Society*, 11 (April 3, 1920), 391–400.
Advocates organization and collective bargaining but not labor affiliation.

269. Quinn, Nellie Marie. "Sabbatical Leave for Chicago School Teachers." *American Teacher*, 13 (May, 1929), 17–18.
A sabbatical leave program for Chicago school teachers has been operating without extra cost to the taxpayers since July, 1927.

270. "Report of Committee on Workers' Education." *American Federation of Teachers Semi-Monthly Bulletin*, 2 (January 20, 1923), 1–2.
The AFT endorses Brookwood Labor College.

271. "Report of the Delegate of California Locals to the Twelfth Annual Convention of the A.F. of T." *American Teacher*, 13 (September, 1928), 30–31.
Discusses the Seattle case and other issues.

272. Rood, Florence. "It's the First Step that Counts." *American Teacher*, 12 (October, 1928), 28–29.
The St. Paul Women's Federation campaigns for salary increases.

273. "R.O.T.C. in Public Schools Is Opposed by A.F. of T." *American Federation of Teachers Monthly Bulletin*, 5 (December, 1925), 1+.
A review of convention resolutions, 1916–1922.

274. Russell, James E. "Organization of Teachers." *Educational Review*, 60 (September, 1920), 129–135.
"It would be a mistake . . . for teachers to form an offensive and defensive alliance [with the AFL]."

275. "Sabbatical Leave of Absence." *American Teacher*, 12 (May, 1928), 20.
Chicago Board of Education approves guidelines for sabbatical leaves of absence for Chicago Teachers.

276. "St. Louis Board of Education and the Unions." *School and Society*, 11 (March 27, 1920), 375–376.
The St. Louis Board bans union membership.

277. Satterthwaite, W. B. "What Seattle Has Been Doing." *American Teacher*, 13 (April, 1929), 1–2.
The fight against the "yellow-dog" rule.

278. _____. "What the N.E.A. Did for Seattle." *American Teacher*, 13 (November, 1928), 15–17.
Charges that NEA leadership sabotaged teacher unity.

279. Schwarztrauber, E. E. "The Portland Teachers' Union." *American Teacher*, 11 (June, 1927), 5–6.
A review of Local 111 activities since 1919.

280. Scott, W. J. "The Technique of the Job." *American Teacher*, 12 (March, 1928), 10–11.
Stresses union cooperation with the school board to improve the quality of education.

281. "Seattle." *American Teacher*, 12 (June, 1928), 3–6.
Support for Seattle teachers voiced by other AFT locals.

282. "The Seattle School Board and the Teachers' Union." *School and Society*, 28 (July 7, 1928), 11.
A discussion of the "yellow-dog" contract.

283. "The Seattle School Case and a Court Decision." *American School Board Journal*, 77 (July, 1928), 56.
A report on the decision upholding the school board in dismissing union teachers.

284. "Seattle to Date." *American Teacher*, 13 (September, 1928), 4–5.
Local 200 goes underground.

285. "The School Executive Looks at the Teachers' Federation." *Nation's Schools*, 3 (March, 1929), 43–46.
Despite admissions of AFT accomplishments, a school administrator expresses an overwhelming preference for the NEA.

286. "Should Teachers Organize?" *School and Society*, 13 (April 30, 1921), 533–535.
Calls for teacher control of educational policy, noting that social class concern over education is nothing new.

287. "The Single Schedule for Those Having Equal Experience, Preparation, and Other Qualifications." *American Teacher*, 11 (January, 1927), 14–15.
Equal pay for equal work for both male and female teachers in all levels of education.

288. Smith, H. P. "How Far Can Teachers' Organizations Go and Be Professional?" *Midland Schools*, 34 (April, 1920), 279–281.
Criticizes labor affiliation.

289. Stecker, Freeland G. "AFT Writes a Decade of History." *American Federation of Teachers Monthly Bulletin*, 5 (April, 1926), 1–4.
A history of federation locals since 1911, written in commemoration of the union's tenth anniversary.

290. _____. "The Issue of Salaries for Men." *American Teacher*, 9 (October, 1920), 161–163.
Advocates equal pay for teachers and good salaries for all.

291. Stillman, Charles B. "The American Federation of Teachers." *American Teacher*, 13 (May, 1929), 4–5+.
An address in honor of William J. Bogan, Chicago superintendent of schools.

292. _____. "The American Federation of Teachers." *Educational Review*, 60 (September, 1920), 120–128. Reply by Arthur O. Lovejoy, *Educational Review*, 60 (November, 1920), 329–335. See also Charles B. Stillman, "The American Federation of Teachers," *American Teacher*, 9 (November, 1920), 182–186.
Stillman contends that the AFT promotes democracy, disavows strikes and the closed shop. Lovejoy rejects labor affiliation for educators.

293. _____. "The Seventh Convention: President Stillman's Report." *American Federation of Teachers Semi-Monthly Bulletin*, 3 (September 20, 1923), 3–4.
Stillman's final presidential address.

294. _____. "The Tax Suits of the Chicago High School Teachers' Federations." *American Teacher*, 11 (April, 1927), 18–19.
The continuing fight for equitable assessments.

295. "Subversion of Public Education; Lusk Laws." *New Republic*, 29 (February 1, 1922), 259–262. Also in *American*

Federation of Teachers Semi-Monthly Bulletin, 1 (February 5, 1922), 3–4.

"The Lusk laws are the conning tower of a lurking submarine" bent upon the destruction of America's free political system.

296. Sutton, Willis A. "Relation of Superintendent to Teachers Association, Atlanta, Georgia, Public Schools." *American Teacher*, 12 (March, 1928), 9–10.

The superintendent of a large city school system stresses sympathy for the teachers' union.

297. Taylor, Boyd. "Fulton County (Georgia) Teachers Association." *American Teacher*, 12 (March, 1928), 14–15.

An account of Local 183 since 1921.

298. "Teachers and Labor Unions." *School and Society*, 25 (January 29, 1927), 138–139.

Advocates teachers' strikes.

299. "Teachers' Tenure Has Consistent Support of A.F. of T." *American Federation of Teachers Monthly Bulletin*, 5 (November, 1925), 1+.

Excerpts from convention resolutions, 1916–1925.

300. "The Teachers' Union." *School and Society*, 11 (January 3, 1920), 27–28.

By refusing to strike, unions rise above "demagoguery and Bolshevism."

301. "Teaching Not a Profession in Seattle." *American Teacher*, 12 (April, 1928), 19–22.

A series of four short articles on Local 200.

302. "The Twelfth Annual Convention of the American Federation of Teachers." *American Teacher*, 13 (September, 1928), 3–4.

The threat posed by the Seattle case is the dominant question at Chicago.

303. "What Brookwood Means." *Nation*, 127 (September 12, 1928), 241.

Support for the labor college in a dispute with AFL Vice President Matthew Woll.

304. "Why a Teachers' Union." *American Teacher*, 13 (May, 1929), 15-17.
    Charles Stillman, Dr. John Lapp, *et al.*, at a meeting of the Elementary Teachers' Union of Chicago, Local 199, reaffirm the AFT objective of freeing the public schools of control by special interests.

305. "Why McAndrew Failed: A Statement by Chicago Locals 2 and 3." *American Teacher*, 12 (May, 1928), 3-6.
    A controversial former superintendent.

306. Williams, Isabel, *et al.* "Out St. Paul Way." *American Teacher*, 13 (February, 1929), 14-16.
    Comments concerning salaries, tenure, and school programs.

307. Wood, Charles W. "Prof. John Dewey on the Hysteria Which Holds Teaching in Check." *American Federation of Teachers Semi-Monthly Bulletin*, 2 (November 5, 1922), 1-2.
    Dewey expresses concern over New York's Lusk laws, but has confidence in the teachers' union.

1930-1941

308. Aaronson, Phyllis, *et al.* "In Defense of Public Education." *American Teacher*, 25 (February, 1941), 16-22.
    AFT campaigns in Detroit, Madison, Chicago, and St. Louis.

309. "Academic Freedom and Tenure: Yale University." *AAUP Bulletin*, 23 (May, 1937), 353-382. Condensed in *School and Society*, 45 (June 12, 1937), 828-829.
    The dismissal of Jerome Davis.

310. "The A.F. of T. Denounces Communism, Fascism, and

Dictatorships." *School and Society*, 52 (August 31, 1940), 136.
A report on the 1940 convention split over the Communist issue.

311. "A.F. of T.'s 20th." *Time*, 28 (August 31, 1936), 35.
Communist and CIO sympathies are said to cloud the 1936 convention.

312. "AFT Committee Chairmen Announce '41 Plans." *American Teacher*, 25 (October, 1940), 8–12.
Ten reports, including academic freedom and pensions.

313. "Answer of Local 5 to Charges Made Against It by the Executive Council." *American Teacher*, 25 (February, 1941), 9–11.
Local 5 spokesman contends that any local disagreeing with the council is in danger.

314. Augustine, Paul. "Trade Teachers in New York." *American Teacher*, 15 (February, 1931), 5.
A brief history of Local 24, the New York Vocational Teachers' Council.

315. "Authority of Boards of Education to Refuse to Employ Teachers Who Are Members of Teachers' Unions." *Elementary School Journal*, 31 (March, 1931), 481–483.
A legal discussion.

316. Axelrod, Donald. "How 'Red' Is the Teachers' Union? Fellow Travelers Lose Control But Liberalism Remains Unshaken." *Common Sense*, 9 (February, 1940), 20–22.
A discussion of the response of the AFT leadership to scurrilous attacks by critics.

317. Barker, Mary C. "Address of President Mary C. Barker." *American Teacher*, 15 (October, 1930), 1–3.
A call for a second full-time officer to aid the secretary-treasurer.

318. Bengtson, Caroline. "Is the American Federation of

Teachers a Labor Union?" *School and Society*, 40 (July 7, 1934), 15–17.
Urges use of the strike and other union weapons.

319. _____. "Superfluous and Detrimental Organization." *School and Society*, 51 (February 24, 1940), 249–250.
Calls for disbanding the AFT for not conforming with labor union methods.

320. Bergman, Walter G. "In Lieu of Proxy Voting: A Suggested Procedure for A.F.T. Conventions." *American Teacher*, 21 (November–December, 1936), 23–24.
Suggests subsidizing convention delegates to insure proportional representation.

321. Besdine, Matthew. "The Rating System: An Anti-Union Weapon." *American Teacher*, 20 (March–April, 1936), 14–15.
A dispute between Local 5 and a New York principal.

322. "A Bid for Unity: Jerome Davis Writes to William Green." *American Teacher*, 22 (November–December, 1937), 22–23.
Davis argues for an AFL–CIO merger.

323. Borchardt, Selma M. "Eradicate Illiteracy! Don't Conceal It." *American Teacher*, 15 (October, 1930), 14–16.
Urges support for a federal education bill to establish remedial reading programs.

324. _____. "Report of the Legislative Representative." *American Teacher*, 16 (December, 1931), 5–6.
Proposals for educational and social welfare bills.

325. _____. "Teachers of the World Meet." *American Teacher*, 16 (October, 1931), 18+.
A Denver conference of the World Federation of Education Associations.

326. Borchardt, Selma M. and Abraham Lefkowitz. "Essentials of a Sound Tenure Law." *American Teacher*, 16 (December, 1931), 8.
A nine-point definition.

327. Brameld, Theodore B. "Karl Marx and the American Teacher." *Social Frontier*, 2 (November, 1935), 53–56.
Regards a Marxist viewpoint as logical for teachers who desire radical social change.

328. "California Organizes: A Symposium on Teacher Organizations." *American Teacher*, 21 (September–October, 1936), 19–21.
Excerpts of speeches on the propriety of union membership.

329. Callis, H. A. "The Negro Teacher and the AFT." *Journal of Negro Education*, 6 (April, 1937), 188–190.
Calls the AFT one of the most democratic and progressive unions with regard to blacks.

330. "The Case of Mr. Vederman." *American Teacher*, 21 (January–February, 1937), 15–16.
A Philadelphia grievance case opposing the rating system.

331. "The Case of Professor Jerome Davis." *School and Society*, 44 (December 19, 1936), 813–814. See also *School and Society*, 45 (June 26, 1937), 892–893.
On Davis's dismissal from Yale.

332. Chambers, M. M. "Teachers' Unions and the Law." *Nation's Schools*, 22 (November, 1938), 39–40.
Despite adverse decisions by courts in Ohio, Illinois, and Washington, the author predicts that the right of teacher union membership will be upheld.

333. "The Children's Charter." *American Teacher*, 15 (April, 1931), 4–5.
Compares statements by the White House Conference on Child Health and Protection (November, 1930), with various AFT pronouncements.

334. "A Code for Public Schools and Public School Teachers." *American Teacher*, 18 (October, 1933), 6–8.
The Executive Council's plan to seek financial aid from the National Recovery Administration.

335. "Communism, Fascism, or Democracy." *American Teacher,* 25 (May, 1941), 3–4.

The entire issue is devoted to essays defining the threat of totalitarian movements, without specific reference to the AFT, but written by many of its leading intellectual advocates, among them George S. Counts, Sidney Hook, John Dewey, and Hans Kohn.

336. "Communists and Teachers." *New Republic,* 104 (February 24, 1941), 265.

A report on plans for a referendum on the expulsion of locals 5, 192, 537.

337. "Communists and Unions." *Nation,* 152 (March 1, 1941), 228–229. Replies by Charles J. Hendley, Reinhold Niebuhr, *et al., Nation,* 152 (March 15, 1941), 307–308; *Nation,* 152 (April 12, 1941), 456.

On the charges that Communists control locals 5, 192, 537.

338. Cook, Cara. "Annual Conference of Teachers in Workers' Education." *American Teacher,* 15 (May, 1931), 20–21.

AFT continues to support Brookwood Labor College after the school has lost the endorsement of the AFL.

339. Corpstein, Susie and E. J. Dupuy. "Retrospection, 1919–1931." *American Teacher,* 15 (May, 1931), 1–2.

A brief history of San Francisco Local 61.

340. Counts, George S. "Dare Progressive Education Be Progressive?" *Progressive Education,* 9 (April, 1932), 257–263; comments by eight educators, pp. 264–278.

"The great weakness of Progressive Education is that it has elaborated no theory of social welfare."

341. _____. "The President's Annual Report." *American Teacher,* 26 (October, 1941), 5–10.

Defense of the resolutions barring Communists and Fascists from membership in the AFT.

342. _____. "Teachers and the Class Struggle." *Social Frontier,* 2 (November, 1935), 39–40.

Warns against glossing over social inequity in the schools.

343. Crew, M. C. "The Chicago Teachers Union Makes Medical History." *American Federationist,* 46 (October, 1939), 1076–1080.
Medical insurance provisions in the 1939 Chicago contract.

344. Crosscup, Richard B. "Forging a National Policy." *American Teacher,* 22 (September–October, 1937), 7–9.
Issues raised at the 1937 convention.

345. Davis, Anne S. "Child Labor and the White House Conference on Child Health and Protection." *American Teacher,* 15 (December, 1930), 1–4. See also Selma M. Borchardt, "White House Conference on Child Health and Protection," *American Teacher,* 15 (January, 1931), 16–18.
Discusses AFT support for new standards of child welfare.

346. Davis, George. "As Viewed by the Teachers Union." *Clearing House,* 11 (September, 1936), 14–16. Reply by C. O. Wright, "The Union Would Place Teachers in the Class Conflict," *Clearing House,* 11 (November, 1936), 140–141.
Contains a general statement on the AFT program.

347. Davis, Jerome. "America's Educational Retreat." *Christian Century,* 54 (July 7, 1937), 868–869. See also *Department of Secondary School Principals Bulletin,* 21 (October, 1937), 53–56.
Charges that corporate interests and poor financing are ruining American education.

348. _____. "Better Schools Called Barrier to Poverty and Fascism in U.S." *American Teacher,* 23 (September–October, 1938), 4.
A presidential address urging equal educational opportunity for American school children.

349. _____. "Teachers and Unemployment." *American Teacher,* 16 (October, 1931), 8+.
Congratulates the union for its realistic approach to social problems.

350. _____. "The Teachers' Struggle for Democracy." *New Republic,* 98 (March 15, 1939), 161–163. Reply by George W.

Hartmann, "Union Teachers and Intellectual Integrity," with a rejoinder by Davis, *New Republic*, 98 (April 26, 1939), 337–341.

A debate over AFT principles in the face of allegations of Communist influence.

351. _____. "Unionization in the College." *Social Frontier*, 3 (November, 1936), 46–48.

Maintains that college instructors need AFT backing in defense of academic freedom.

352. _____. "Why College Teachers Should Join the A.F. of T." *American Teacher*, 20 (March–April, 1936), 19–20.

The AFT as a bulwark of democracy and social progress.

353. _____. "Why the American Federation of Teachers." *American Teacher*, 19 (May–June, 1935), 3–4.

Six proofs of the value of union membership.

354. "Davis' Diplomacy." *Time*, 32 (August 29, 1938), 22.

Jerome Davis is reported to have quieted suspicions of CIO sympathies.

355. DeBriae, Edward C. "The Milwaukee Union Initiates Education for Democracy." *American Teacher*, 19 (November–December, 1934), 5–6+.

A demand for liberalization of the social science curriculum.

356. DeLacy, Hugh. "Retreat to the Mountain." *Social Frontier*, 3 (March, 1937), 174–175.

Black Mountain Workers' College.

357. "Detroit Local Wins Reinstatement of 41 Married Teachers." *American Teacher*, 26 (October, 1941), 27–29.

A Hamtramck, Michigan, case.

358. Dewey, John. "The Crisis in Education." *American Teacher*, 17 (April, 1933), 5–9. Condensed in *AAUP Bulletin*, 19 (May, 1938), 318–319.

Calls the AFT the only organization both strong and worthy enough to defend teacher interests.

359. _____. "The Schools and the White House Conference." *American Teacher*, 16 (February, 1932), 3–4.
"The great lesson which educators have to learn from . . . the White House Conference is an enlarged sense of social responsibility."

360. _____. "The Teacher and the Public." *American Teacher*, 19 (March–April, 1935), 3–4.
"Teachers are workers . . . bound in common ties with all other workers."

361. _____. "United, We Shall Stand." *School and Community*, 21 (April, 1935), 11–12.
"Join (AFT) locals where they exist; help form them where they do not exist."

362. Diamant, Gertrude. "The Teachers' Union." *American Mercury*, 33 (September, 1934), 108–113.
Local 5's fight for academic freedom.

363. Eby, Kermit. "What A Union Can Contribute to Education." *Clearing House*, 13 (March, 1939), 402–415.
Credits the CTF with improving teacher morale and school financing.

364. _____. "What the Chicago Teachers Union Contributes to Education in Chicago." *School and Society*, 51 (May 25, 1940), 670–673. Reply by Caroline Bengtson, *School and Society*, 52 (November 23, 1940), 527–529.
Advocates a broadening of the union program.

365. "Education, Democracy, and Defense: An Analysis, a Statement of Ideals and Principles, and a Program of Action." *American Teacher*, 25 (March, 1941), 5–35. Condensed in *Education Digest*, 6 (May, 1941), 7–10.
A definitive statement of policy by the Executive Council with particular view to the possibility of American entry into World War II.

366. "Educators Urged to Join with Other Workers." *School Management*, 4 (June, 1935), 207.

A summary of John Dewey's argument that the AFT fights against the economic isolation of teachers.

367. Elder, Arthur. "Attacks on Tenure in Michigan." *American Teacher*, 21 (September–October, 1936), 13–15. See also *American Teacher*, 21 (November–December, 1936), 9–10.
Cases from Corunna and Highland Park, Michigan.

368. "The Election in Kellogg." *American Teacher*, 19 (January–February, 1935), 3.
An AFT victory in an Idaho mining community.

369. Everett, R. W. "Education in the California Legislature." *American Teacher*, 15 (May, 1931), 13–14.
Reviews the position of AFT locals on tenure, pension, textbook bills.

370. "The Executive Council's Proposal to Save the AFT." *American Teacher*, 25 (April, 1941), 2+. See also "For a United and Effective AFT—Reply of Locals 5, 192, and 537," *American Teacher*, 25 (April, 1941), 3+.
Official charges of Communist domination of three AFT locals and their defense.

371. "The Fight Against Alleged Communism in the AFT." *School and Society*, 53 (June 14, 1941), 750.
Opposing views on the expulsion of locals 5, 192, and 537.

372. Fisher, Lyman B. "Buffalo Industrial Teachers' Association; Local 39." *American Teacher*, 15 (February, 1931), 11.
The local's relief fund and special aspects of vocational education.

373. Forer, Bernard. "Where a Law Is Not a Law." *American Teacher*, 22 (January–February, 1938), 11–12.
AFT response to tenure law evasion in New Jersey.

374. "Formation at St. Louis of a Local Union of the American Federation of Teachers." *School and Society*, 42 (August 24, 1935), 253–254.
Local 420 fights a "yellow-dog" rule.

375. "Freedom of Contract in Seattle." *American Teacher*, 15 (March, 1931), 10–11.
    The school board abolishes the "yellow-dog" clause in the Seattle teachers' contracts.

376. Grant, E. Allison. "A Valiant Fight: Massachusetts Progressives Unite Against the Loyalty Oath." *American Teacher*, 21 (March–April, 1937), 14–15.
    Labor solidarity pledged to repeal a state law.

377. Green, William. "Green Pledges Full Support to Organize Nation's Teachers." *American Teacher*, 25 (September, 1940), 7–8.
    AFL President William Green calls for a new organizing drive among teachers.

378. _____. "Labor and Education." *American Teacher*, 17 (October, 1932), 7–10.
    Admonishes the AFT, "Build your organization!"

379. Grossman, Mary Foley. "This Year in Washington." *American Teacher*, 22 (May–June, 1938), 8–9.
    AFT lobbying for federal aid to public schools.

380. Groves, Harold M. "The Purpose and Functions of a Teachers' Union in a University." *American Teacher*, 18 (February, 1934), 8–10.
    Attempts to define union responsibilities "in the midst of an attack upon education . . . unparalleled in our history."

381. "Growth in Membership of the American Federation of Teachers." *Elementary School Journal*, 39 (December, 1938), 251.
    A brief report on the doubling of AFT membership.

382. Hand, Harold C. "Answering Objections to the AFT." *American Teacher*, 21 (May–June, 1937), 22–24.
    Objections to the view that the AFT is a disruptive minority among teachers.

383. Hanson, Alice. "Notes on Academic Freedom." *American Teacher*, 25 (January, 1941), 13–15.

Defense of academic freedom in Minnesota, Pennsylvania, and New York.

384. Hardy, Ruth Gilette. "Historical Setting of the American Federation of Teachers." *American Teacher,* 16 (November, 1931), 5–6+.
    Considers the AFT in perspective of sixty years of American education.

385. Harper, C. L. "Jacksonville Wins Tenure." *American Teacher,* 26 (December, 1941), 13–14.
    A new Florida law favors Local 516.

386. "The Hearst Attack on Academic Freedom." *Social Frontier,* 1 (February, 1935), 25–34.
    AFT leaders and their locals are frequently attacked in the newspaper chain's crusade against Communists.

387. Herrick, Mary J. "Midwest Teachers Organize." *American Teacher,* 22 (September–October, 1937), 23–24.
    A successful organizing drive in the Midwest.

388. Hullfish, H. Gordon. "Why I Am Resigning From the Teachers' Union." *Social Frontier,* 3 (January, 1937), 110–112; reply by Elliot M. Grant, pp. 112–113.
    Charges the AFT aligns class against class.

389. Jablonower, Joseph. "The Teachers' Union Completes Fifteen Years of Service." *New Republic,* 66 (March 18, 1931), 130.
    A letter reviews Local 5 history on the occasion of its fifteenth anniversary.

390. _____. "What Does It Profit a Union?" *American Teacher,* 15 (February, 1931), 1–2. Reply by C. L. Vestal, *American Teacher,* 15 (March, 1931), 22–23.
    The AFT has become less responsive to the "rank and file" and more conservative in its outlook.

391. Jaffee, Haym. "Children Strike for Teachers." *American Teacher,* 21 (November–December, 1936), 11–13.
    A Walker County, Alabama, dispute.

392. Jewett, Victor R. "Unprofessional Conduct." *American Teacher*, 20 (May–June, 1936), 15.
Charges against a California teacher.

393. Johnson, Orvel. "Red Mist Over Philadelphia." *National Republic*, 24 (October, 1936), 1-2.
Purports that the 1936 convention is dominated by Communist sympathizers.

394. Kerlin, Robert T. "Unionization of Teachers." *American Teacher*, 18 (February, 1934), 14–15.
An appeal for support from other unions.

395. Kuenzli, Irvin R. "The American Federation of Teachers." *Labor Information Bulletin*, 7 (July, 1940), 4–6.
A survey of the AFT program and membership growth.

396. _____. "Crises in Jacksonville and Toledo." *American Teacher*, 24 (March, 1940), 8–10.
On the mass dismissal of teachers in Florida and a fair contract in Ohio.

397. _____. "The Relation of the Federation of State Programs of Education." *American Teacher*, 19 (May–June, 1935), 9–10.
Proposals drawn from the Ohio Federation of Teachers' program.

398. _____. "The Teachers Union In Action." Mount Morris, Illinois: American Federation of Teachers, 1938–1954.
The annual report of the secretary-treasurer was published in *American Teacher* from 1938 to 1954 under this or similar titles. Kuenzli also wrote a monthly column during those years.

399. "Labor Speaks on Teachers and Unionism." *American Teacher*, 18 (April, 1934), 13–14.
Several state AFL leaders issue supporting statements for the AFT.

400. Landis, Joseph F. "Cleveland Wins Its Pegged Levy." *American Teacher*, 25 (February, 1941), 14–16.

Local 279 contributes to a successful campaign for more school revenue.

401. Langdon, Eunice. "The Teacher Faces the Depression." *Nation*, 137 (August 16, 1933), 182–185.
Particular attention is given to the Local 5 position in the pay crisis.

402. Laski, Harold J. "The Teachers Union in a New Social Order." *American Teacher*, 16 (October, 1931), 10–11+.
A tribute to Henry R. Linville and also to Local 5 on its fifteenth anniversary.

403. Lefkowitz, Abraham. "The AFT Fight for Federal Aid." *American Teacher*, 19 (October, 1934), 4–5.
Calls for "at least as much government assistance as is being given to businessmen."

404. _____. "Crisis in the Teachers' Union." *Nation*, 141 (October 9, 1935), 410–411; reply by the opposition "United Committee to Save the Union," pp. 411–412.
Lefkowitz decries the disruptive tactics of Communists within Local 5.

405. _____. "The Depression and Educational Statesmanship." *American Teacher*, 16 (November, 1931), 10.
Decries salary cuts and layoffs.

406. _____. "The Legislative Program of Local 5, New York." *American Teacher*, 15 (February, 1931), 2–3.
For new pension laws, against attempts to undermine existing teacher benefit legislation.

407. Lewis, Celia and William T. McCoy. "Shall We Affiliate with the CIO?—A Forum for Union Members." *American Teacher*, 22 (September–October, 1937), 12–14. Replies: *American Teacher*, 22 (November–December, 1937), 12; 22 (January–February, 1938), 14–15; 22 (March–April, 1938), 26–27; 22 (May–June, 1938), 24–28.
Contains a proposed resolution for a CIO referendum.

408. Linville, Henry R. "Address of the President." *American Teacher*, 17 (October, 1932), 3–5.

Condemns Depression induced salary cuts. Proposes a more active AFT role within the AFL.

409. _____. "The American Federation of Teachers." *School and Society*, 40 (November 10, 1934), 616–621. Condensed in *AAUP Bulletin*, 20 (December, 1934), 514–515; *School Management*, 4 (April, 1935), 154. Reply by Caroline Bengtson, *School and Society*, 40 (December 22, 1934), 845–846.

A statement of union philosophy, and an answer to objections to labor affiliation.

410. _____. "Bread, Butter, and Ideals." *American Teacher*, 16 (October, 1931), 4–6+.

A presidential address hailing a new social attitude among educators.

411. _____. "The Challenge of the Economic Situation to Organized Teachers." *American Teacher*, 18 (October, 1933), 3–5.

A presidential address concentrating on the commitment of the AFT to social education.

412. _____. "How Communists Injure Teachers' Unions." *Social Frontier*, 5 (March, 1939), 173–176. Reply by Charles J. Hendley, "Unionism in the Educational Field," *Social Frontier*, 5 (May, 1939), 237–240.

An indictment of Local 5 for "Stalinist" politics.

413. _____. "Some Union Jobs." *American Teacher*, 15 (February, 1931), 4–5.

Argues that economic depression affords no excuse for union laxity.

414. _____. "Yellow-Dog Contracts for Teachers." *Nation*, 133 (July 1, 1933), 13–14.

Illinois, Ohio, Washington, and other states use contracts forbidding union membership for teachers.

415. "Local No. 1." *Time*, 30 (November 8, 1937), 34.

A report on the founding of the CTU amidst corruption scandals in the Chicago schools.

416. "Louisville AFT Defends Education." *American Teacher,* 26 (November, 1941), 15–17.
Attempts to eliminate race and sex discrimination in salaries.

417. Lowry, Raymond F. "United for Democracy in Education and the Nation." *American Teacher,* 20 (September–October, 1935), 3–6.
A presidential address focusing on improving job security.

418. Lyons, Marian C. "The Value of the Union Movement to Chicago Teachers." *American Teacher,* 14 (April, 1930), 10–12.
Discussion of the recent programs of both the women's and men's locals and why they remain separate.

419. McAndrew, William. "Appraising Radical Teachers' Unions." *School and Society,* 35 (February 6, 1932), 191–192. Reply by Henry R. Linville, "The President's Page," *American Teacher,* 16 (June, 1932), 14–15. See also William McAndrew, "A Basis for Appraising Teachers Unions," *School and Society,* 35 (April 23, 1932), 564–566.
Debate over whether the AFT works for the welfare of society or strictly for the welfare of teachers. Linville affirms that the union fights for the good of all.

420. Mayer, Milton S. "When Teachers Strike: Chicago Learns Another Lesson." *Forum and Century,* 90 (August, 1933), 121–125.
The Chicago teachers' "riot" of 1933.

421. Menefee, Seldon C. "Northwest Teachers on the March." *American Teacher,* 22 (September–October, 1937), 20–21.
AFT growth in Washington, Oregon, and Montana.

422. Minton, Bruce. "The Plot against the Teachers." *New Masses,* 37 (November 12, 1940), 15.
A sympathetic view of Local 5 under fire.

423. Newlon, Jesse H. "The A.F. of T. Moves Forward." *Frontiers of Democracy*, 7 (October 15, 1940), 6.
Hails the union for its progressive anti-Communist stance.

424. "No Seats for Reds." *Time*, 38 (September 1, 1941), 70.
On the aftermath of expulsion of locals 5, 192, and 537.

425. "Organized Teachers Speak Out." *New Republic*, 88 (September 9, 1936), 118.
A report on the 1936 convention.

426. Peterson, Esther, et al. "A Symposium on Organization." *American Teacher*, 21 (March–April, 1937), 10–13. See also Martin Rugg, "Symposium on Organization—2," *American Teacher*, 21 (May–June, 1937), 12–15.
Regional leaders discuss plans for growth.

427. "Placing the Responsibility." *American Teacher*, 17 (December, 1932), 3.
Criticizes the Chicago School Board and the financial community for the neglect of education and of teachers.

428. Preisler, Paul W. "St. Louis Local Wages a Winning Fight for the Right to Organize." *American Teacher*, 21 (May–June, 1937), 17.
A school board imposed anti-union rule is repealed.

429. "A Program for 1940 Adopted by the National Executive Council of the AFT." *American Teacher*, 24 (February, 1940), 6–9.
Opposes budget cuts, attacks on civil liberties, and the possibility of US entry into World War II.

430. "A Program of Objectives." *American Teacher*, 18 (December, 1933), 4–5.
The 1933 convention adopts a statement urging the American public to halt the deterioration of the schools resulting from the Depression.

431. "Promotion and Organization." *American Teacher*, 17 (October, 1932), 22–23.
One of a series of reports from the 1932 convention.

432. "The Purge in the AFT." *New Republic*, 104 (June 16, 1941), 809–810.
Report on the expulsion of locals 5, 192, and 537.

433. Randolph, Vance. "Utopia in Arkansas." *Esquire*, 9 (January, 1938), 60+.
A report on Commonwealth College, debunking the myth that Commonwealth is a hotbed of free love and subversion.

434. "Reds Routed." *Time*, 37 (June 16, 1941), 43.
Report on the expulsion of locals 5, 192, and 537.

435. "Refusal of Public School Board to Employ Union Teachers Does Not Violate Constitutional Rights." *Law and Labor*, 13 (January, 1931), 5–6.
The 1930 Washington State Supreme Court decision in the Seattle "yellow-dog" case.

436. "Report on the Committee for Industrial Organization and the American Federation of Labor." *American Teacher*, 22 (January–February, 1938).
Issued as a thirty-six-page supplement, the report contains information on CIO membership and the implications for the AFT should the AFT decide to affiliate with the CIO.

437. "San Francisco Administrators' Federation, Local 215." *American Teacher*, 15 (May, 1931), 12.
A principals' and supervisors' local, founded in 1930.

438. "The San Francisco Teachers' Salary Survey, Local 61." *American Teacher*, 15 (May, 1931), 2.
Regarding the local's finances, 1930–1931.

439. Schendel, Gordon. "Minneapolis Fights 10-Year Cut." *American Teacher*, 26 (December, 1941), 7–8.
Discusses ten-fold membership increases and the first substantial salary improvement in a decade.

440. "Scholarship and the Ministry." *Christian Century*, 54 (June 9, 1937), 736–737.
On the dismissal of Jerome Davis from Yale.

441. Schwartztrauber, E. E. "The Seattle Election." *American Teacher*, 14 (April, 1930), 12–13.
The defeat of pro-union candidates for school board positions.

442. _____. "A Worker's Summer School." *American Teacher*, 15 (November, 1930), 11-15.
Report on the Wisconsin Summer School for Workers in Industry.

443. Shukotoff, Arnold. "A Program of Defense." *American Teacher*, 22 (November–December, 1937), 7–9.
Urges protection for teachers against unfair rulings by administrators and school boards.

444. _____. "Progress in Cooperation: The AFT and AAUP." *American Teacher*, 20 (May–June, 1936), 18–19.
Argues that the two organizations are complementary.

445. _____. "Yale Corporation *vs.* Freedom: Jerome Davis Discharged by Vested Interests." *American Teacher*, 21 (November–December, 1936), 5, 9.
A discussion of the Davis case, with letters of support from members of the Yale faculty and others.

446. Smith, C. Currien. "Should Teachers Organize as a Trade Union?" *School and Society*, 53 (January 4, 1941), 25-27; reply by Abraham Tauber, pp. 416–418; rejoinder by Smith, pp. 789–791.
Smith charges that the AFT is antagonistic to the spirit of public education. Tauber defends the union.

447. Smith, Stanton. "Chattanooga Fights for Better Schools." *American Teacher*, 25 (February, 1941), 12–14. Successes reported, *American Teacher*, 26 (October, 1941), 13–14.
Local 246 loses a round in the contest for tenure and better salaries but has some success to report.

448. Smith, Stanton, *et al.* "A Communication to Local Unions of the A.F. of T." *American Teacher*, 20 (March–April, 1936), 10–12.

Views, pro and con, on proposed convention voting changes which would strengthen the voice of larger locals.

449. "The Social Policy of the American Federation of Teachers." *Nation's Schools*, 8 (December, 1931), 70–71.
An editorial charging that union teachers seek "personal benefit" above "professional growth."

450. Starr, Mark. "Trebled Membership Seen Result of Ouster of Stalinite Officials From Teacher's Union." *New Leader*, 23 (September 7, 1940), 5–6.
Victorious progressives at the Buffalo convention.

451. Stolberg, Benjamin. "Communist Wreckers in American Labor." *Saturday Evening Post*, 212 (September 2, 1939), 5–7+.
Charges that Communists control the AFT.

452. "Students on Strike." *Nation*, 136 (January 4, 1933), 19–20. See also a fourth letter, *Nation*, 136 (April 26, 1933), 476.
Three letters regarding a dispute at Commonwealth College, Mena, Arkansas.

453. "Teachers in Hague Territory." *American Teacher*, 22 (March–April, 1938), 7–8.
The union *vs.* the Jersey City, New Jersey, political machine.

454. "Teachers: Jerome Davis Leans to CIO, Embarrasses Yale." *Newsweek*, 10 (September 6, 1937), 19.
A report charging that the AFT neglects educational issues.

455. "The Teachers Union Controversy." *Social Frontier*, 2 (October, 1935), 24–25. See also *Social Frontier*, 2 (November, 1935), 56–57.
Key position papers by Henry Linville and others on the 1935 split within Local 5.

456. "Teachers Union Defeated in Seattle." *School Review*, 38 (May, 1930), 329–330.
"Yellow-dog" contracts are upheld by the Washington Supreme Court.

457. "Teachers Unions and the American Federation of Labor." *School and Society*, 49 (January 28, 1939), 110.
Locals 5, 453, and 537 are suspended by the Central Trades and Labor Council of New York for Communist domination.

458. "Teachers Unions in the Headlines." *American Teacher*, 20 (May–June, 1936), 5–6.
Reports on AFT victories in Memphis, St. Louis, Cleveland, and other cities.

459. "Teachers View a Sit-Down." *American Teacher*, 21 (January–February, 1937), 19.
The Flint (Michigan) Federation supports the UAW-CIO sit-down strike of 1936–1937.

460. "Trade Union of Chicago Teachers." *School and Society*, 46 (November 20, 1937), 665-666.
The merger of four Chicago locals as the CTU, Local 1.

461. "The Twenty-Fifth Annual Convention." *American Teacher*, 26 (October, 1941), 3–4.
Resolutions against membership in the AFT for adherents of totalitarian movements.

462. "Two Horse." *Time*, 30 (September 6, 1937), 66+.
A report on the dispute over CIO sympathies at the 1937 convention.

463. "Two Statements by the National Executive Council of the AFT." *American Teacher*, 25 (January, 1941), 3–5.
The expulsion of Local 5.

464. Umstattd, J. G. "Teachers Associations, Organizations, and Unions." *Review of Educational Research*, 7 (June, 1937), 314–315.
A brief review of AFT membership statistics, with a bibliography of literature published 1934–1936.

465. Wakeham, G. "Should College Teachers Join the AFT?"

School and Society, 54 (November 15, 1941), 441–443. Reply by Joseph W. Cohen, "Should College Teachers Join the AFT? —A Reply to Professor Wakeham," *School and Society*, 55 (February 14, 1942), 190–193. Discussion by Tyrus Hillway, "Labor Unions and the Teaching Profession—A Reply to Mr. Cohen," *School and Society*, 55 (May 2, 1942), 505–506.

Questions whether college professors have the courage to withstand the pressure from the opponents of organized labor.

466. Walsh, Sara T. "Pennsylvania Wins Tenure." *American Teacher*, 21 (May–June, 1937), 19–21.
The AFT helps to pass a tenure bill.

467. Ward, Harry F. "Civil Liberty for Teachers." *American Teacher*, 15 (October, 1930), 3–4.
Urges the defense of individual teachers discriminated against because of union activity.

468. Weber, Addie L. and Bernard Forer. "The Case of Thirteen Teachers." *American Teacher*, 26 (December, 1941), 9–12.
A defense of academic freedom in Trenton, New Jersey.

469. Wechsler, James. "Twilight at Teachers College." *Nation*, 147 (December 17, 1938), 661–663. Replies: George S. Counts, "Whose Twilight?" *Social Frontier*, 5 (February, 1939), 135–140; Charles J. Hendley, "Unionism in the Educational Field," *Social Frontier*, 5 (May, 1939), 237–240.
Discussion concerning the influence of Communists within the AFT. Counts declares that the AFT disavows any connection with Communists. The Local 5 position is argued by Hendley, who charges that red-baiting of union members is disrupting the Columbia University education faculty.

470. Weil, Dorothy. "The Chicago Situation." *American Teacher*, 16 (October, 1931), 12–13.
Chicago locals protest salary cuts and payment in scrip.

471. Wells, George K. and Clayton Black. "The Peru, Indiana

Tenure Case." *American Teacher*, 25 (January, 1941), 15–16.
Local federation goes to court to defend salary levels and tenure.

472. "Who's in the Union?" *Time*, 37 (February 3, 1941), 68.
Report outlines charges of Communist domination of Local 5.

473. "Yale on Trial: Two Documents in the Case of Jerome Davis." *New Republic*, 89 (November 18, 1936), 85–92.
The official statement given to the press by Yale University and a report on the case by a panel of professors from other institutions protesting Davis's dismissal.

1942–1949

474. "AFT and NEA on Teachers' Pay." *America*, 76 (January 18, 1947), 427.
Praises the AFT for urging state and federal aid to schools.

475. "AFT Reverses Itself." *America*, 77 (September 6, 1947), 623. Reply by William E. McManus, *America*, 77 (September 20, 1947), 700.
Regrets an AFT decision not to support aid to private schools.

476. "Alaska's First AFT Local Is Organized." *American Teacher*, 30 (May, 1946), 16–18.
Ketchikan Local 868.

477. Borchardt, Selma M. "Report of AFT's Washington Representative." *American Teacher*, 31 (October, 1946), 27–32. See also *American Teacher*, 31 (April, 1947), 5–9.
Reviews the official AFT position on federal aid to education.

478. _____. "S717, the AFT–AFL Federal Aid Bill, and Other

Federal Legislation." *American Teacher*, 29 (April, 1945), 4–6.
A summary and a comparison of legislation which is also supported by the NEA.

479. _____. "Should the Public School System Be Subsidized by Federal Funds?" *Congressional Digest*, 25 (February, 1946), 53+.
US Senate testimony in favor of a bill providing federal aid to private as well as public schools.

480. Bray, William C. "Rhode Island's New Retirement System." *American Teacher*, 33 (April, 1949), 13–15.
A statewide contributory retirement system for teachers.

481. Bremfoerder, Alice. "Toledo Wins Full Restoration." *American Teacher*, 27 (January, 1943), 5.
Local 250 averts a pay cut.

482. Butler, Wayne C. "The Oglesby Incident." *Nation's Schools*, 44 (November, 1949), 26+. See also "Coercion of Oglesby School Board Told by Threatened Members," *Nation's Schools*, 45 (January, 1950), 28–32.
A Tri-Cities, Illinois, strike in support of a fired teacher.

483. Capen, Samuel P. "The Teaching Profession and Labor Unions." *Journal of General Education*, 1 (July, 1947), 275–278. Condensed in *Education Digest*, 13 (November, 1947), 19–21.
"Teachers, as teachers, should not join labor unions."

484. Counts, George S. "The Retiring President's Report to the Gary Convention." *American Teacher*, 27 (October, 1942), 5–8.
A five-point program for the war years.

485. _____. "Socio-Economic Forces in Teachers' Strikes." *Phi Delta Kappan*, 28 (April, 1947), 350+.
Contends unionization is a sign of professional maturity.

486. Creel, Warren. "He's In, You're Out—The Duluth Tenure Cases." *American Teacher*, 23 (February, 1943), 7–8.
A tenure law upheld, but plaintiffs still denied their positions.

487. Cross, E. A. "Time for a Teachers' Union." *School and Society*, 61 (April 21, 1945), 241–243. Discussion, *School and Society*, 62 (July 7, 1945), 11; *School and Society*, 62 (August 4, 1945), 78–80. Condensed in *Education Digest*, 10 (May, 1945), 16–18.
Justification for a strong national teachers' union.

488. Derbigny, I. A. "Labor Unionism in American Colleges." *School and Society*, 69 (March 5, 1949), 172–174.
A survey indicates that 1.7 percent of faculty nationwide were members of AFL affiliated locals in 1947.

489. "Do Teachers Have the Legal Right to Strike?" *American School Board Journal*, 114 (May, 1947), 27–28+.
Opposing views of two New Jersey attorneys. Ooetje John argues that the strike is an effective, legal weapon for teachers, while Harold D. Green states that teachers do not have the legal right to strike.

490. Eby, Kermit. "Labor's Program for Teachers in the Post-War World." *Teachers College Record*, 47 (October, 1945), 38–42. Condensed in *Education Digest*, 11 (January, 1946), 17–19.
Argues that unionization would improve the teacher's social status.

491. _____. "Teachers' Unions and School Administration." *American School Board Journal*, 104 (June, 1942), 20–21.
A general statement of union philosophy.

492. Eklund, John M. "The American Federation of Teachers." *Phi Delta Kappan*, 31 (October, 1949), 66–70.
A short history of AFT programs and goals.

493. _____. "Critical Problems Facing the AFT." *American Teacher*, 34 (October, 1949), 7–9.
A presidential address dealing with questions such as academic freedom and school funding.

494. _____. "Promotion—the 'Super Rating.'" *American Teacher*, 32 (April, 1948), 11–12.
On promotion as a reward for subservience.

495. Fewkes, John M. "The Crisis in Education." *American Federationist*, 50 (March, 1943), 10–12.
AFT policies and goals benefit school children above all.

496. _____. "The President's Message to the Membership." *American Teacher*, 27 (October, 1942), 30–31.
An endorsement of George S. Counts's wartime program for the AFT.

497. _____. "Uphill Struggle All the Way: The First Ten Years of the Chicago Teachers Union." *American Federationist*, 55 (February, 1948), 18–20.
A general statement on the CTU program, 1937–1947.

498. Fordyce, Wellington G. "The American Federation of Teachers—Its History and Organization." *American School Board Journal*, 112 (June, 1946), 23–26.
Concentrates on issues of the 1930s, indicating that the AFT grew more conservative as a result of the turmoil over Communist influence.

499. _____. "The Historical Background of American Teacher Unions." *American School Board Journal*, 112 (May, 1946), 43–44.
A brief survey of AFT history up to the 1920s and an examination of union claims of accomplishment since then.

500. _____. "Teachers' Unions and Labor's Weapons." *American School Board Journal*, 113 (September, 1946), 31–33.
Supports the official AFT "no strike" position, but warns that inadequate salaries could force the union to change its position.

501. Graham, James D. "Union Teacher in Helena, Montana, Dismissed Without Statement of Cause or Hearing." *American Teacher*, 30 (October, 1945), 23–24.
The case receives national AFT consideration.

502. Gregg, Russell T. and Roland A. Koyen. "Teacher Associations, Organizations, and Unions." *Review of Educational Research*, 19 (June, 1949), 260–264.
A survey of the literature, 1940–1949.

503. Guernsey, George T. "Rockford Ends Its Blackout." *American Teacher*, 26 (January, 1942), 7–10.
Discussion of new school revenues for an Illinois community.

504. Hartung, Maurice L. "Strikes by Teachers." *School Review*, 54 (December, 1946), 563–566. Condensed in *Education Digest*, 12 (March, 1947), 29–31.
A philosophical discussion of the strike issue.

505. Herrick, Mary. "Subjective Rating for Teachers." *American Teacher*, 32 (April, 1948), 9–10.
Rejects merit ratings.

506. "High School Students and the Manpower Shortage." *Education for Victory*, 2 (November 1, 1943), 20.
A report on a wartime AFT resolution urging industry to hire women and retirees rather than high school students to replace men lost to the military.

507. Hooser, Edmund. "Chattanooga Teachers Receive Salary Increase." *American Teacher*, 27 (February, 1943), 9–10.
On raises for both black and white teachers.

508. Kochman, P. "Teacher Organizations on Strikes." *Phi Delta Kappan*, 28 (April, 1947), 353–354.
A brief comparison of AFT and NEA positions.

509. Kuenzli, Irvin R. "Company Unions and the School Crisis." *American Federationist*, 54 (February, 1947), 10–12.
The NEA is responsible for low teacher salaries.

510. _____. "Interesting Facts from AFT History." *American Teacher*, 30 (May, 1946), 6–8.
A short summary marking the thirtieth anniversary of the union.

511. _____. "Organized Teachers Fight for Democracy." *American Federationist*, 53 (May, 1946), 17–19.
Calls the AFT vital in the fight against anti-union indoctrination in the public schools.

512. Landis, Joseph F. "The AFT Today." *American Teacher*, 33 (October, 1948), 2+.
Presidential address at the 1948 Glenwood Springs, Colorado, convention discusses the teacher shortage and the strengthening of state federations.

513. _____. "American Education and the AFT Program." *American Teacher*, 31 (October, 1946), 2+.
Presidential address focuses on the need for better school funding.

514. _____. "Angry Americans." *American Federationist*, 53 (December, 1946), 18–19.
Maintains that low teacher pay cheats American youth.

515. Lane, Layle. "Report of the Committee on Cultural Minorities of the American Federation of Teachers." *Journal of Negro Education*, 14 (January, 1945), 109–112.
Union policy recommendations in areas of human relations, employment, law enforcement, and political democracy.

516. MacKenzie, Stewart. "Teachers' Strikes, a Professional Disgrace." *Nation's Schools*, 40 (July, 1947), 54.
Anti-strike article.

517. " 'Merit' Rating—What's Wrong With It? New York's AFT Members Give the Answer." *American Teacher*, 33 (April, 1949), 7–8.
A protest against the endorsement of merit rating by the American Association of University Women in New York.

518. Motter, Alton M. "Crisis in Public Education." *Christian Century*, 64 (January 29, 1947), 140–141.
An interpretation of the background of the St. Paul Federation strike in 1946.

519. Nathanson, Jerome. "John Dewey and the Twentieth Century." *Labor and Nation*, 5 (July–August, 1949), 6–8.
Commemoration of Dewey's ninetieth birthday, concentrating on his contributions to educational philosophy.

520. Oliver, Clarence E. "Portland Wins Salary Increase." *American Teacher*, 26 (March, 1942), 14–15.
Factors contributing to Local 111's successful salary campaign.

521. Parsons, E. Dudley, Jr. "Minneapolis AFT Prevents Decrease in Final Salary Payment." *American Teacher*, 27 (January, 1943), 6.
The local cites a violation of the state salary stabilization act by the school board.

522. Redmond, James. "Teachers Are Striking." *Phi Delta Kappan*, 28 (April, 1947), 351–352.
A brief survey of strikes in the early post-World War II period.

523. Reeves, Floyd. "Current Educational Problems and the Work of the AFT Commission on Educational Reconstruction." *American Teacher*, 31 (October, 1946), 12–19.
Report of the work in progress of the AFT Commission on Education and the Postwar World.

524. _____. "The Report of the AFT Commission on Educational Reconstruction." *American Teacher*, 32 (October, 1947), 16–17.
Definition of desirable goals for American education.

525. "Report on Action Taken by the AFT Executive Council Following Its Investigation of Three Locals." *American Teacher*, 33 (February, 1949), 5–9.
The expulsion of Los Angeles Local 430 and University of Washington Local 401 for Communist influence. Reforms reported at San Francisco Local 61.

526. Robinson, Clarence B. "Local 428 Gains Salary Victory." *American Teacher*, 26 (January, 1942), 10–11.
A victory for the black teachers' local in Chattanooga.

527. "The St. Paul Story." *American Teacher*, 31 (February, 1947), 8–9.
A strike for higher salaries and better school conditions.

528. "The St. Paul Strike." *American School Board Journal,* 114 (January, 1947), 62.
     While "not a proper weapon," strikes could force school boards to readjust salary schedules.

529. Simonson, Rebecca. "Teacher Rating and Teacher Morale." *American Teacher,* 32 (April, 1948), 8.
     Opposes merit ratings.

530. Starr, Mark. "John Dewey the Social Activist." *Labor and Nation,* 5 (July–August, 1949), 8–9.
     Hails Dewey's support for the AFT and other organizations dedicated to reform.

531. "Struck Buffalo." *Newsweek,* 29 (March 3, 1947), 22.
     A strike by the Buffalo Teachers' Federation.

532. "Summary of Action Taken by the AFT Executive Council at Its Meeting in Chicago, December 28–30, 1948." *American Teacher,* 33 (February, 1949), 3–4+.
     A resolution encouraging affiliation of black locals in Louisiana.

533. "Teacher Strike." *Newsweek,* 31 (March 8, 1948), 80.
     A brief report on the Minneapolis strike, 1948.

534. "Teacher Strikes." *School and Society,* 65 (April 19, 1947), 277.
     Report of official NEA policy adopted in 1947 stressing that teacher strikes can be avoided by effective "collective group negotiation."

535. "Teachers Set Wage Minimum." *American Federationist,* 54 (January, 1947), 7.
     A report on an AFT goal of $2,500 as a minimum teacher salary.

536. "A Teachers' Strike." *American School Board Journal,* 113 (October, 1946), 54.
     An editorial reaction to a strike by Norwalk, Connecticut, teachers, questioning whether the AFT might change its no-strike policy.

537. "Teachers' Union and Board of Education Sign Collective Bargaining Agreement." *American Teacher*, 29 (November, 1944), 6–11.
A model contract for Cicero, Illinois.

538. "Teachers Union Straddles Parochial Aid Issue." *Christian Century*, 64 (September 10, 1947), 1068.
A report on the reaction of Catholic school authorities to the AFT position on federal aid to education.

539. "Toward Better Race Relations in Detroit." *American Teacher*, 32 (February, 1948), 13–16.
On the role of the Detroit local in the city's "Intercultural Committee."

540. Turley, Ira S. "Full Salary Restored to Chicago after Ten Years." *American Teacher*, 27 (February, 1943), 5–6.
Six raises in six years bring teachers to the 1929 salary levels.

541. "Union Convention Highlights." *Nation's Schools*, 42 (August, 1948), 51.
A report on the 1948 convention.

542. "Union Demands Decent Schools: Local 59, Minneapolis." *American Teacher*, 26 (February, 1942), 4–7.
A major funding crisis.

543. "The War and Education: A Statement by the AFT Executive Council." *American Teacher*, 26 (January, 1942), 3–6.
The AFT response to the US entry into World War II.

544. "Working Agreement between Bremerton Local and Bremerton, Washington, School Board." *American Teacher*, 31 (May, 1947), 23–25.
An early collective bargaining agreement.

545. "AFL-CIO Calls NEA Company Union." *American Teacher*, 42 (February, 1958), 11.
AFL-CIO convention resolution.

546. "A.F. of T. Joins 69 Organizations to Solve Children's Problems." *American Teacher*, 1 (January, 1955), 5.*
The AFT is represented at a Health, Education, and Welfare conference.

547. "AFT Active at Midcentury White House Conference." *American Teacher*, 35 (January, 1951), 5–7; *American Teacher*, 35 (February, 1951), 10–13.
Union positions on vocational training, housing, ADC.

548. "AFT Airs the Bus Issue." *America*, 83 (September 9, 1950), 570.
Discusses AFT opposition to use of public funds for transportation of parochial school students.

549. "AFT Desegregation Complete." *American Teacher*, 5 (September, 1958), 1–2.
The voiding of the last racially segregated local's charter.

550. "AFT Drive On." *Senior Scholastic*, (Teacher Supplement), 69 (September 27, 1956), 3.
A report on the 1956 convention.

551. "AFT Executive Council Establishes Area Field Service, States Policy on Strikes." *American Teacher*, 36 (February, 1952), 8–9.
AFT reaffirms "no-strike" policy.

---

* In January 1955 the AFT began publication of a newspaper, *The American Teacher*, which alternated monthly with its magazine of the same name. The magazine continued its run of volume numbers, but the newspaper began as volume 1. The last issue of the magazine (volume 49) appeared in April 1965. In September 1965 the newspaper began to be issued monthly (beginning with volume 12). In September 1966 the newspaper adopted the volume numbering system from the magazine (beginning with volume 51).

552. "AFT Executive Council Takes Action to Terminate Services of Secretary-Treasurer." *American Teacher*, 38 (April, 1954), 16.
Irvin R. Kuenzli is fired and his duties are assumed by President Carl J. Megel.

553. "AFT Files *Amicus Curiae* Brief in Segregated Schools Case." *American Teacher*, 38 (February, 1954), 14.
Urges "integrated schooling on every level."

554. "AFT Makes Gains." *Senior Scholastic*, (Teacher Supplement), 71 (September 20, 1957), 4.
A report on the 1957 convention.

555. "AFT Survey Shows Teachers' Tenure in 48 States." *American Teacher*, 3 (November, 1956), 1+.
Defines "a good tenure law" for states.

556. "American Federation of Teachers Votes Not to Defend Any Teacher Proved to be a Communist." *Nation's Schools*, 50 (October, 1952), 124+.
A report on the 1952 convention.

557. Barbash, Jack. "Bargaining for Professionals and Public Employees." *American Teacher*, 43 (April, 1959), 7–8+.
A noted labor scholar argues that solidarity is the only means of achieving full professional recognition.

558. Borchardt, Selma M. "Should Federal Subsidies Be Given Students for Higher Education?" *Congressional Digest*, 34 (August, 1955), 212+.
Congressional testimony favoring federal scholarships, loans, and college subsidy funds.

559. Carey, Hope V. "Arbitration Added to Pawtucket Contract." *American Teacher*, 2 (March, 1956), 8.
A two-year contract won by Rhode Island Local 930.

560. Caylor, Marie L. "A.F. of L. Launches Organization of

Nation's Teachers." *American Teacher,* 39 (February, 1955), 5–6.

The AFL promises backing for a campaign to double AFT membership.

561. "Censors L.A. Teachers." *American Teacher,* 3 (March, 1957), 1–2.

The Los Angeles superintendent bans "political circulars," including AFT bulletins, in schools.

562. "Chicago, Detroit Urge Teachers Protection." *American Teacher,* 1 (January, 1955), 6.

Local leaders say that teachers cannot control the increasing amount of violence in urban schools.

563. Cohen, Morris. "AFT Fights Segregation in Suit before U.S. Supreme Court." *American Teacher,* 34 (February, 1950), 19–20.

The AFT files *amicus curiae* briefs in Texas and Oklahoma.

564. "Collective Bargaining *vs.* Collective Begging." *American Teacher,* 41 (October, 1956), 11–12.

A convention panel acquaints delegates with collective bargaining rights.

565. Connelly, Mary. "Kenosha Teachers Win A Raise in Photo Finish." *American Teacher,* 40 (December, 1955), 9–10.

Local 577 benefits from united labor backing.

566. "Contract between the Eau Claire Local and the Eau Claire Board of Education." *American Teacher,* 34 (May, 1950), 7–9.

Wisconsin Local 696's contract for 1949 published as a model.

567. Corey, Paul. "Cleveland's Local 279 Becomes of Age." *American Teacher,* 1 (May, 1955), 6+.

Reviews the local's twenty-one-year history.

568. "Eight Southern Locals Told to Integrate before 1958." *American Teacher,* 3 (September, 1956), 5.

One of three reports on the directive to end segregation within the AFT.

569. Filiere, Clarence. "Cleveland, 279, Opposes Merit Rating Plan." *American Teacher*, 5 (January, 1959), 12.
A survey indicates discontent among Cleveland teachers.

570. Fitzpatrick, James L. "Wisconsin Maps Legislation for State Aid, Pensions." *American Teacher*, 1 (January, 1955), 7.
Proposals for pension reform.

571. "Gags San Francisco Teachers." *American Teacher*, 1 (March, 1955), 1–2. See also Douglas Stout, "Legislature Takes Gag Rule Off San Francisco Teachers," *American Teacher*, 2 (September, 1955), 1–2.
School board bans teacher participation in political campaigns.

572. Garber, Lee O. "Are 'Union Shop' Contracts for Teachers Legal?" *Nation's Schools*, 61 (February, 1958), 70–71. See also "Supreme Court of Montana Rules Against Teachers' Union," *Nation's Schools*, 64 (September, 1959), 57–58.
A district court ruling permits the continued employment of non-union teachers.

573. "Good Publicity Helps Win Salary Campaign." *American Teacher*, 35 (November, 1950), 5–6.
Well-written ads produced by Local 833, New Jersey.

574. Hatchett, E. W. and Carl F. Maedl. "A.F. of T. Locals in the Canal Zone." *American Teacher*, 40 (February, 1956), 11–12.
On the Balboa Local 227 and Atlantic Local 228.

575. "Hawaii Enacts AFT Legislation." *American Teacher*, 6 (September, 1959), 1–2.
Representation obtains raises and improved working conditions.

576. "Idaho Teachers Made Goats in School Discipline Fiasco." *American Teacher*, 1 (May, 1955), 7.
Pocatello Local 1087 charges that teachers are not responsible for disorder in overcrowded and understaffed schools.

577. "Indiana Local Wins a War." *American Teacher*, 4 (November, 1957), 1–2.
A victory over a Terre Haute school board trustee.

578. Irwin, Edward A. "Los Angeles Plan Helps Teachers, Pupils, Taxpayers." *American Teacher*, 1 (January, 1955), 7.
Adoption of a paid sick-leave policy.

579. Irwin, Edward A., et al. "So! You Want to Get Out a Newspaper." *American Teacher*, 40 (December, 1955), 7–8.
The experience of AFT local editors in Detroit, Los Angeles, Portland, and other cities.

580. Jablonower, Joseph. "John Dewey Memorial Address." *American Teacher*, 37 (November, 1952), 12–16.
Reviews the relationship between Dewey's educational philosophy and his constant support of the AFT.

581. Jellison, John F., et al. "Foundations for a Profession." *American Teacher*, 41 (December, 1956), 9–10+.
The founding of five new locals.

582. Jewett, Edward T. "An A.F. of T. Local in the Corn State: the Saga of 738." *American Teacher*, 40 (October, 1955), 13–14.
The Council Bluffs Federation founded in 1943.

583. Justin, Florence. "The Bremerton Story." *American Teacher*, 40 (February, 1956), 5–6.
Local 336 is voted bargaining agent in Washington.

584. Karr, Sam P. "Breakdown in Teaching Requirements." *American Teacher*, 41 (April, 1957), 7–8.
Protests the continued hiring of non-degree teachers.

585. Krause, Rosalie C. "An A.F. of T. Leader Talks to School Boards." *American Teacher*, 42 (April, 1958), 7–8+.
An Illinois official addresses the old professionalism question.

586. Labb, Margaret. "Gary, Local 4, Wins the Right to Negotiate." *American Teacher*, 40 (October, 1955), 7–8+.
A strike threat wins board recognition and a pay raise.

587. Leipold, L. E. "High Living Costs Cause Teacher Unrest on the Salary Front." *American School Board Journal*, 121 (December, 1950), 27–28+.
      Advocates six preventive measures against strike situations.

588. _____. "A Summary of the Minneapolis School Strike: Who Really Won?" *American School Board Journal*, 122 (April, 1951), 31–32.
      The strike of January–February, 1951, advanced as an argument for compulsory arbitration.

589. Levitan, Sar A. "Professional Organization of Teachers in Higher Education." *Journal of Higher Education*, 22 (March, 1951), 123–128.
      AFT's influence among college faculties is minimal.

590. Lieberman, Myron. "Some Reflections on Teachers Organizations." *Educational Forum*, 24 (November, 1959), 71–76.
      A survey of weakness in teachers' organizations.

591. _____. "Teacher Strikes: An Analysis of the Issues." *Harvard Educational Review*, 26 (Winter, 1956), 39–70.
      Favors the right to strike so long as no better means of bargaining exists.

592. Ligtenburg, John. "AFT Policy with Respect to Communist Teachers and the Fifth Amendment." *American Teacher*, 38 (February, 1954), 4–7.
      Denies any contradiction between forbidding Communists membership and the defense of a teacher for invoking the Fifth Amendment.

593. _____. "Defense of Tenure, Teachers' Rights." *American Teacher*, 41 (December, 1956), 5–6+.
      A review of the AFT Defense Fund.

594. _____. "Right of Public Employees to Bargain Collectively." *American Teacher*, 35 (April, 1951), 14–15.
      The Minnesota Supreme Court upholds the right of public employees to strike.

595. _____. "A Teachers' Attorney Evaluates the 'Loyalty Oath.'" *American Teacher*, 41 (February, 1957), 13–14+.
Asks for repeal of laws requiring loyalty oaths.

596. _____. "Teachers' Unions and Next Year's Legislatures." *American Teacher*, 43 (December, 1958), 11–12.
Urges well-planned efforts before the various state legislatures.

597. Lyle, Floyd, *et al.* "How Teachers' Unions and Central Labor Councils *Are* Working Together to Open a New Era in Teacher–Employer Relations." *American Teacher*, 41 (October, 1956), 9–10+.
Examples from California, Wisconsin, Michigan, and Washington.

598. McGill, Margaret E. "Teachers Have Human Rights." *America*, 85 (August 4, 1951), 439.
Defense of a strike by Pawtucket (Rhode Island) Local 930 in 1951.

599. "Massachusetts Strengthens Tenure." *American Teacher*, 5 (September, 1958), 1–2.
Tenure and collective bargaining legislation is enacted.

600. Meany, George. "Why Teachers Belong in the AFL-CIO." *American Teacher*, 42 (December, 1957), 9+.
Stresses mutual benefits of the AFT and labor.

601. "Meany Backs A.F. of T. Non-Segregation Policy After Atlanta Secedes." *American Teacher*, 41 (February, 1957), 12+.
The AFL-CIO president approves a firm integration stand adopted at the 1956 convention.

602. Megel, Carl J. "The Nation's School Problem" *American Federationist*, 60 (September, 1953), 17+.
Stresses the importance of labor affiliation.

603. _____. "Not Enough Teachers." *American Federationist*, 66 (September, 1959), 10–11+.
Emphasizes AFT goals for quality education.

604. _____. "The Problem of Education." *American Federationist*, 65 (July, 1958), 13–15.
Discusses the broad AFT program of member services.

605. _____. "A Teacher Union Leader Views School Problems." *Teachers College Record*, 59 (October, 1957), 26–31. Condensed in *Education Digest*, 23 (January, 1958), 22–25.
Outlines the AFT response to problems caused by the teacher shortage.

606. _____. "Teachers Belong in the Labor Movement." *American Federationist*, 63 (May, 1956), 17.
A brief argument for teacher vigilance.

607. _____. "Who Teaches Your Children?" *American Federationist*, 64 (August, 1957), 16–17+.
Discusses the range of teacher salaries to illustrate union effectiveness.

608. Megel, Carl J., *et al.* "Goals of the American Federation of Teachers: A Symposium by Executive Council Members Sums Up Our Objectives for Teachers of America." *American Teacher*, 40 (April, 1956), 5–6+.
Calls for adequate salaries, collective bargaining, tenure, professional certification, pensions, academic freedom, federal aid to education.

609. "Megel Calls for Action Program." *American Teacher*, 3 (September, 1956), 1+.
Carl J. Megel is re-elected president, calls for a $5,000 minimum salary for teachers.

610. "Megel Urges Schools for New Age." *American Teacher*, 5 (May, 1959), 1–2.
Calls for enactment of the Murray-Metcalf Aid Bill.

611. "Minnesota Enacts Teachers Bargaining Law." *American Teacher*, 4 (September, 1957), 1+.
Legislation enforcing collective bargaining.

612. Minnis, Lemuel E. "When Chicago Teachers Need a Loan."
American Teacher, 1 (January, 1955), 11.
Reviews the history of Local 1's credit union.

613. Nelson, Mercedes L. "The Minneapolis Story." *American Teacher*, 41 (April, 1957), 11–12+.
A history of Minneapolis locals 59 and 238.

614. Philley, Flora A. "Tenure Case Won by Local 4." *American Teacher*, 35 (February, 1951), 19–22.
A Gary, Indiana, teacher's job is threatened for protesting racial segregation.

615. "Reuther Urges Less Talk, More Action." *American Teacher*, 4 (September, 1957), 1–2.
AFT convention address by UAW President Walter P. Reuther.

616. Rippa, S. Alexander. "The Textbook Controversy and the Free Enterprise Campaign, 1940–1941." *History of Education Journal*, 9 (Spring, 1958), 48–58.
Relates how the National Association of Manufacturers promoted a censorship campaign directed at school textbooks containing a liberal viewpoint.

617. Roach, Stephen F. "School Boards and Teacher Strikes." *American School Board Journal*, 135 (November, 1957), 54.
New Hampshire Supreme Court rules that teacher strikes for salary increases are illegal.

618. Roth, Herrick S. "Colorado Fights Faceless Informers." *American Teacher*, 39 (December, 1954), 5–6+.
The state federation is joined by Denver's press in demanding fair hearings for accused teachers.

619. "The Salary Difficulties in Garfield, New Jersey." *American Teacher*, 38 (February, 1954), 15–18.
Report on a short successful strike.

620. Schiff, Albert. "Teachers' Strikes in the United States." *Phi Delta Kappan*, 34 (January, 1953), 133–135.
Strikes have attracted needed attention to underfinanced schools.

621. Schnitzler, William F. "A Labor Leader Talks to Teachers." *American Teacher*, 40 (October, 1955), 5–6.
AFL-CIO secretary-treasurer discusses the AFT's position within the newly united AFL-CIO.

622. Schwanke, Marie L. and Sylvia J. Solomon. "How Local 250 Became a Majority Union." *American Teacher*, 39 (December, 1954), 13+.
Good public relations and AFL backing produced a successful union of Toledo teachers.

623. "Shall the Basis of Electing Delegates to AFT Conventions Be Changed?" *American Teacher*, 38 (April, 1954), 12–14.
A proposal to permit a fairer representation for larger locals.

624. Shlakman, Vera. "White Collar Unions and Professional Organizations." *Science and Society*, 14 (Summer, 1950), 214–236.
Judges the AFT to be "relatively weak."

625. Simpson, Helen L. and Louis W. Filliger. "An A.F. of T. Local under the Northern Lights." *American Teacher*, 41 (February, 1957), 9–10+.
Anchorage (Alaska) Local 1175.

626. "Spirited Debate on Basic Issues Features AFT Convention in Peoria." *American Teacher*, 38 (October, 1953), 4–13.
Delegates express concern about charges of Communist influence and the taking of the Fifth Amendment.

627. Starr, Mark. "Meet Workers Education Local 189 of the A.F. of T." *American Teacher*, 41 (October, 1956), 15–16.
An introduction to the workings of Local 189.

628. Stecker, Freeland D. "How the A.F. of T. Began." *American Teacher*, 41 (April, 1957), 13–14.
From the 1956 convention address of the former AFT secretary-treasurer.

629. "Teachers and Collective Bargaining: An Analysis of the Issues." *NEA Research Bulletin*, 36 (April, 1958), 46–49.
A survey of state legislation across the U.S. pertaining to teachers' unions.

630. "Teachers Before Legislatures." *American Teacher*, 3 (January, 1957), 1–2.
A survey of the legislative petitions of ten state federations.

631. "Teachers Hold Meeting." *American Federationist*, 59 (August, 1952), 24.
A brief report on the 1952 convention.

632. "Teachers Union Says Eisenhower Administration Delay on School Construction Costly for Future." *Nation's Schools*, 54 (October, 1954), 150+.
A report on the 1954 convention.

633. "Unite for Federal Aid." *American Teacher*, 3 (January, 1957), 1+.
AFT and AFL-CIO leaders organize a federal conference on school aid.

634. Varnum, Walter C. "ETV—Messiah or Monster?" *American Teacher*, 43 (October, 1958), 9–10+.
Warns that television is no substitute for professional classroom techniques.

635. Ward, Paul D. "Are We Selling Children Down the River?" *American Teacher*, 5 (March, 1959), 10.
Calls for increased federal aid to education.

636. Williamson, Roger. "School's Out in Pawtucket." *Nation*, 172 (June 16, 1951), 561–562.
Pawtucket, Rhode Island, strike of 1951.

637. Yabroff, Bernard and Lily Mary David. "Collective Bargaining and Work Stoppages Involving Teachers." *Monthly Labor Review*, 76 (May, 1953), 475–479.
A review of work stoppage policies before the 1950s.

1960–1965

638. "AFL-CIO Aids AFT Organization." *American Teacher,* 46 (March, 1962), 1–2.
The AFT joins the AFL-CIO Industrial Union Department on recommendation of Walter Reuther.

639. "AFT Elects Cogen." *Senior Scholastic,* (Teacher Supplement), 85 (September 23, 1964), 1+.
A report on the 1964 convention.

640. "AFT Offices to Famous Mansion." *American Teacher,* 45 (March, 1961), 1–2; *American Teacher,* 45 (May, 1961), 1+.
The McCormick house in Chicago becomes union headquarters.

641. "AFT Sets Goals." *Senior Scholastic,* (Teacher Supplement), 77 (September 21, 1960), 2.
A report on the 1960 convention.

642. "Alliance of AFT and AFL-CIO." *Michigan Education Journal,* 42 (April, 1965), 6–10.
Charges that labor affiliation for teachers is an "unholy marriage."

643. "American Federation of Teachers: What It Wants, How It Bargains, Where It's Headed." *School Management,* 8 (February, 1964), 56–58.
An interview with David Selden, touching on professionalism, rivalry with the NEA, strikes, and other matters.

644. Baker, Ellis T. "Do's and Don'ts in Union Press Relations." *American Teacher*, 49 (December, 1964), 7–8.
    Advice from the editor of the American Newspaper Guild's *Guild Reporter*.

645. Berube, Maurice R. "Problems of Teacher Unionism." *New Politics*, 4 (Fall, 1965), 37–42.
    Views the resurgence of the AFT as part of "a new age of commitment," which began with the civil rights movement.

646. Betchkal, James. "NEA and Teacher Unions Bicker and Battle for Recognition." *Nation's Schools*, 74 (August, 1964), 35–41+. Condensed in *Education Digest*, 30 (November, 1964), 12–15.
    A survey of major school districts by state and region.

647. "Big Little Man." *Newsweek*, 62 (September 2, 1963), 71.
    A brief report on the election of Charles Cogen as AFT president.

648. Birnbaum, Elliot. "Who Speaks for Teachers?" *IUD Digest*, 7 (Summer, 1962), 42–49.
    On the Empire State Federation of Teachers fight for Social Security, annuity reform, and collective bargaining rights.

649. Bleeker, Ted. "New York City's Effective Schools Make History." *American Teacher*, 49 (April, 1965), 5–6.
    On the beginnings of the More Effective Schools (MES) Program by the UFT.

650. Bloom, Arnold M. "A More Militant Profession." *American School and University*, 37 (October, 1964), 17.
    An editorial warning superintendents of growing AFT influence.

651. Borchardt, Selma M. "The A.F. of T. Aid Program in Washington." *American Teacher*, 45 (April, 1961), 7–8+.
    Calls for tax reforms and Social Security hikes as well as school aid.

652. "Boston Teachers Union Wins Election." *American Teacher,*
12 (November, 1965), 3.
AFT local defeats a non-labor affiliated association.

653. Bowen, John J. "Better Working Conditions, Better Education." *American Teacher,* 45 (February, 1961), 13–14.
Tactics concerning non-salary issues.

654. Brinckman, William W. "Teachers' Organizations and Labor
Unions." *School and Society,* 89 (March 11, 1961), 96+.
Editorial criticizes labor affiliation.

655. Brooks, George. "A Case for Teachers' Unions." *Monthly
Labor Review,* 87 (March, 1964), 292. Replies: Sidney Dorros,
"The Case for Independent Professional Teachers' Asso-
ciations," *Monthly Labor Review,* 87 (May, 1964), 543; John
M. Glasgow, "More on Teachers," *Monthly Labor Review,*
88 (May, 1965), 535; Sidney Dorros, "And in Conclusion,"
Monthly Labor Review, 88 (May, 1965), 536.
Brooks considers the AFT to be "the natural recourse for
teachers who want their interests made known."

656. Brooks, Thomas R. "Handwriting on the Blackboard."
Commonweal, 76 (May 4, 1962), 142–143. Reply by Albert J.
LaMothe, Jr., with rejoinder, *Commonweal,* 76 (June 1, 1962),
256–257.
Predicts an upsurge in teacher unionism following the
success of the early UFT strikes.

657. Bruce, William C. "An Illegal Strike." *American School
Board Journal,* 144 (June, 1962), 44.
Editorial calls the UFT strike of April 11, 1962, "unprofessional" and "destructive" but acknowledges its effectiveness.

658. Buder, Leonard. "The Teachers Revolt: Report from New
York City." *Phi Delta Kappan,* 43 (June, 1962), 370–376.
UFT strike of 1962 with a review of major editorial opinion.

659. Caliguri, Joseph. "Do Associations and Unions Have

the Same Goals?" *American School Board Journal*, 147 (December, 1963), 9–10.

This article, based on the author's dissertation, states that there is less difference between the AFT and the NEA than is commonly believed.

660. Carey, James B. "A Labor Leader Warns the National Education Association." *American Teacher*, 47 (October, 1962), 11–12.

A controversial lecture by an AFL-CIO vice-president illustrating the greater effectiveness of the AFT.

661. Carr, William J. "The Assault on Professional Independence." *Phi Delta Kappan*, 46 (September, 1964), 17–18; see also Carl J. Megel, "The AFT Reply: Which Organization Gets Results?" 19–21.

Carr, NEA executive secretary, presents views. Megel charges that "class snobbery and fear are at the base of the vicious anti-union attack."

662. Cherry, Howard L. "Negotiations between Boards and Teacher Organizations." *American School Board Journal*, 146 (March, 1963), 7–9.

A comparison of AFT strikes and NEA "sanctions."

663. "Chicago Teachers Win CB Election Rights and Salary Hike." *American Teacher*, 12 (October, 1965), 3.

Local 1 beats a strike deadline.

664. "Church and State: AFT *vs.* NEA over Federal Aid to Parochial Schools." *Senior Scholastic* (Teacher Supplement), 85 (December 2, 1964), 6.

Report discusses AFT support for federal aid to parochial schools.

665. Cogen, Charles. "Blueprint for Democracy in Teacher Bargaining." *American Teacher*, 12 (September 15, 1965), 4+.

Urges a joint AFT–NEA program for establishing collective bargaining rules.

666. ———. "Departure from the Old Ways: The First Year of New York City Bargaining." *American Teacher*, 48 (October, 1963), 5–6+.

The first UFT president discusses the use of strikes.

667. ———. "To Revive a Dying School System." *American Teacher*, 48 (October, 1963), 7+.

UFT collective bargaining strategy.

668. "Cogen New AFT President." *American Teacher*, 11 (September, 1964), 1+.

Charles Cogen's career is outlined; Albert Shanker succeeds him at the UFT.

669. Cohodes, Aaron. "How New York's Gross Lives and Learns with Unions." *Nation's Schools*, 74 (November, 1964), 47–49.

The New York City school superintendent speaks of his dealings with the UFT.

670. "Connecticut, Michigan Improve Teacher CB Rights." *American Teacher*, 12 (September 15, 1965), 9–10.

Gains in two states contrasted with restrictive legislation in California and New Jersey.

671. Corey, Arthur M. "Strikes or Sanctions?" *NEA Journal*, 51 (October, 1962), 13–15.

Calls strikes inappropriate, unprofessional, illegal, outmoded, and ineffective.

672. Corwin, Ronald G. "Militant Professionalism, Initiative, and Compliance in Public Education." *Sociology of Education*, 38 (Summer, 1965), 310–331.

Study indicates a high correlation between professionalism and militancy.

673. Dashiell, Frederick K. "We Have Learned Strategic Lessons." *Michigan Education Journal*, 42 (April, 1965), 12–14.

NEA rationalizes the loss of elections to the AFT in Detroit and Cleveland.

674. Dawson, George G. "Doctoral Studies on the Relationship between the Labor Movement and Public Education."

Journal of Educational Sociology, 34 (February, 1961), 260–269.

Reviews of nine dissertations, several of which discuss the AFT's role in the development of labor support for public education.

675. DeMars, Robert. "Michigan Wins Mediation." *American Teacher,* 6 (January, 1960), 1–2.

A state court upholds the Labor Board's jurisdiction over teacher disputes.

676. "Detroit Election Winner." *American Teacher,* 10 (June, 1964), 1–2.

The report includes tabulations of all major representation elections to date.

677. Doherty, Robert E. "Attitudes toward Labor: When Blue-Collar Children Become Teachers." *School Review,* 71 (Spring, 1963), 87–96.

Study alleges that teachers from union family background show antipathy towards professional union membership.

678. Donovan, Bernard, *et al.* "Collective Bargaining *vs.* Professional Negotiations." *School Management,* 9 (November, 1965), 68–75.

Charles Cogen's views are reported as representative of the AFT.

679. "Drive to Unionize School Teachers." *U.S. News and World Report,* 53 (July 16, 1962), 76–77.

The NEA is reported as alarmed by the AFT.

680. "Drives Against Rating." *American Teacher,* 8 (March, 1962), 1–2.

On a national meeting on the theme, "Merit Rating—Educational Cancer."

681. Elam, Stanley M. "Collective Bargaining and Strikes? Or Professional Negotiations and Sanctions?" *Phi Delta Kappan,* 44 (October, 1962), 1–11. Condensed in *Education Digest,* 28 (January, 1963), 1–4.

A comparison of the "classic" AFT and NEA positions.

Argues that teachers must be goal oriented, not organization oriented.

682. _____. "Teacher Power—Product of Unification and Bigness." *Phi Delta Kappan*, 45 (March, 1964), 269.

Editorial stresses that only the "organized strength" of teachers can make the profession attractive.

683. _____. "Teachers' Unions: Rift Without Differences." *Nation*, 201 (October 18, 1965), 247–249.

Attempts to summarize and minimize the difference between the AFT and the NEA.

684. _____. "Union or Guild? Organizing the Teachers." *Nation*, 198 (June 29, 1964), 651–653. Revised text, "Who's Ahead, and Why: The AFT–NEA Rivalry." *Phi Delta Kappan*, 46 (September, 1964), 12–15.

On the AFT–NEA rivalry.

685. Epstein, Benjamin. "What Status and Voice for Principals and Administrators in Collective Bargaining and 'Professional Negotiation' by Teacher Organizations?" *National Association of Secondary School Principals Bulletin*, 49 (March, 1965), 226–259.

Administrators should fight unions to protect their own interests.

686. Exton, Elaine. "NSBA Opposes Teachers' Strikes and Sanction." *American School Board Journal*, 146 (June, 1963), 41+.

The National School Boards Association's position on AFT and NEA militancy.

687. Fewkes, John M. "The Dawn of a New Era for Teachers." *American Teacher*, 48 (October, 1963), 13–14.

Status of collective bargaining recognition in Chicago.

688. "Fiasco in Hamtramck." *Michigan Education Journal*, 42 (May 1, 1965), 4.

Calls the 1965 AFT strike in Hamtramck, Michigan, "illegal" and "irresponsible."

689. Fitzpatrick, James L. "Problems of A.F. of T. Locals."
American Teacher, 45 (February, 1961), 7–8+.
Discusses local organizational structure, finances, and newsletters.

690. Gould, Sidney C. "A History of the New York City Teachers Union and Why It Died." *Educational Forum*, 29 (January, 1965), 207–215.
The expulsion of Local 5 and its subsequent rivalry with the AFT Teachers Guild.

691. Groff, Patrick J. "Teacher Organizations and School Desegregation." *School and Society*, 90 (December 15, 1962), 441–442. Condensed in *Education Digest*, 28 (March, 1963), 5–7.
Praises AFT support of the civil rights movement.

692. "Guild and High School Teachers Merger Voted." *American Teacher*, 44 (April, 1960), 20.
The birth of the UFT in New York City.

693. "Hamtramck Gets Pact with Sit-Down." *American Teacher*, 11 (June, 1965), 1–2.
A Michigan local wins results with the first teacher sit-down strike.

694. Hechinger, Fred M. "The Story behind the Strike." *Saturday Review*, 45 (May 19, 1962), 54+.
Author sees no long range benefits from the 1962 UFT strike.

695. Hixson, Richard A. "Battle for Bargaining in the Smoke of River Rouge." *American Teacher*, 49 (December, 1964), 9–10.
Taylor (Michigan) Local 1085.

696. Hopkins, John. "A Review of Events in Professional Negotiations." *Theory into Practice*, 4 (April, 1965), 51–54.
AFT–NEA rivalry.

697. "In California, AFT Pushes Fight Against Winton Law." *American Teacher*, 12 (November, 1965), 8–9.

Protests against a law establishing negotiation councils that would also handle administrators' salaries.

698. Ingerman, Sidney. "Employed Graduate Students Organize at Berkeley." *Industrial Relations*, 5 (October, 1965), 141–150.
The organization and programs of University of California Local 1570, representing graduate students.

699. "Inside of Teachers Union." *American School and University*, 36 (November, 1963), 42–46+.
AFT gains during Carl Megel's administration.

700. "Institute Faculty Wins." *American Teacher*, 11 (June, 1965), 1–2.
Strike by the Faculty Federation of the Art Institute of Chicago.

701. Klass, Irwin. "The New Breed of Teacher: Ferment in the Ranks Breaks Old Stereotype." *American Federationist*, 69 (November, 1962), 1–5.
Teachers potential for increased public service has been advanced by the AFT.

702. Krider, Donald. "A Teacher and a Labor Union." *Wisconsin Review*, 2 (Summer, 1963). Reprinted in *Contemporary Labor Issues*, Walter Fogel and Archie Kleingartner, ed. (Belmont, California: Wadsworth Publishing Co., 1966), pp. 262–266.
A Madison, Wisconsin, teacher speaks for the AFT membership.

703. "Labor Trouble Ahead for Schools?" *U.S. News and World Report*, 57 (September 7, 1964), 75.
Brief report on an AFT organizing drive.

704. Langer, Howard. "Scholastic Teacher Interviews Carl J. Megel." *Senior Scholastic*, (Teacher Supplement), 83 (October 4, 1963), 24–26.
Megel discusses AFT history, labor affiliation, and other matters.

705. _____. "Scholastic Teacher Interviews Charles Cogen."

Senior Scholastic (Teacher Supplement), 85 (November 4, 1964), 7–8.
Cogen discusses union philosophy and plans for the future.

706. Lieberman, Myron. "The Battle for New York City's Teachers." *Phi Delta Kappan,* 43 (October, 1961), 2–8. Condensed in *Education Digest,* 27 (December, 1961), 13–16. Reply by Robbins Barstow, Jr., *Phi Delta Kappan,* 43 (December, 1961), 118–124.
Predicts that UFT success will have national implications for teacher unionism.

707. _____. "Teachers Choose a Union." *Nation,* 193 (December 2, 1961), 443–447+.
An analysis of the issues that brought about the merger of teacher organizations in New York City.

708. _____. "Teachers on the March: The Militant Mice." *Nation,* 200 (February 1, 1965), 107–110.
Examines teacher strikes and causes.

709. _____. "Teachers' Strikes: Acceptable Strategy?" *Phi Delta Kappan,* 46 (January, 1965), 237–240.
Strikes are but one part of the crisis of independent school funding.

710. _____. "Who Speaks for the Teachers?" *Saturday Review,* 48 (June 19, 1965), 64–66+.
Favors an AFT–NEA merger provided the membership is protected from "organizational abuses."

711. Lobenthal, Martin. "The UFT–NYC Board of Education Agreement—A Teacher's View." *Theory into Practice,* 4 (April, 1965), 66–69.
Study of the 1965 strike and the significance of UFT strength.

712. "Los Angeles Federation Urges Reduction of Class Size in the Riot Area." *American Teacher,* 12 (September 15, 1965), 6+.
Response to the Watts riot of 1965.

713. Lowe, William T. "Who Joins Which Teachers' Group?" *Teachers College Record*, 66 (April, 1965), 614–619. Condensed in *Education Digest*, 31 (October, 1965), 10–12.

Survey indicates that "dissatisfied" teachers are more likely to join AFT than NEA.

714. Lunden, Leon E. "The 1964 Convention of the Teachers Union." *Monthly Labor Review*, 87 (October, 1964), 1138–1142.

The presidential election, organizing, recognition, and other related matters are discussed.

715. Megel, Carl J. "Can a Case Be Made for Teachers' Unions?" *Nation's Schools*, 73 (February, 1964), 51+.

"The teacher obtains a voice . . . the administrator can locate real grievances."

716. _____. "Merit Rating Is Unsound: The AFL-CIO Position." *Phi Delta Kappan*, 42 (January, 1961), 154–156. See also *American Teacher*, 45 (February, 1961), 19–20+.

Seniority-based salary scales, tenure, and increased fringe benefits are the basis of the AFL-CIO program for organized school teachers.

717. _____. "Teacher Conscription—Basis of Association Membership?" *Teachers College Record*, 66 (October, 1964), 7–17. Reply by Marion L. Steet, "Professional Associations— More than Unions," *Teachers College Record*, 66 (December, 1964), 203–218. See also Michael Moskow, "Teacher Organizations: An Analysis of the Issues," *Teachers College Record*, 66 (February, 1965), 453–463.

Charges that administrations have "conscripted" teachers into the NEA.

718. _____. "The Union Pattern in Teachers' Organizations." *Teachers College Record*, 63 (November, 1961), 115–120.

Emphasizes labor's traditional commitment to educational reform.

719. _____. "Your Right to Choose Your Organization." *American Teacher*, 10 (January, 1964), 6.

Teachers coerced into the education associations.

720. "Milwaukee Union Strengthens Membership for Re-Challenge." *American Teacher*, 10 (March, 1964), 3.
Milwaukee Local 252 loses to its NEA rival.

721. Moskow, Michael H. "Collective Bargaining for Public School Teachers." *Labor Law Journal*, 15 (December, 1964), 787–794.
Finds "no significant difference" between the collective bargaining procedures of the AFT and the NEA.

722. _____. "Recent Legislation Affecting Collective Negotiations for Teachers." *Phi Delta Kappan*, 47 (November, 1965), 136–141.
Developments in California, Connecticut, Michigan, Oregon, Washington, and Wisconsin.

723. _____. "Teacher Organizations: An Analysis of the Issues." *Teachers College Record*, 66 (February, 1965), 453–463.
Argues that the AFT has set the trend for teachers' organizations in the 1960s.

724. "NEA Frowns at Merger Talk, but Teacher Union Smiles at It." *Nation's Schools*, 76 (December, 1965), 58.
Charles Cogen's views as to why no merger was imminent.

725. "Negotiating with Teachers." *School Management*, 9 (May, 1965), 81–87+.
Includes a summary of a 1964 arbitration settlement with Eau Claire (Wisconsin) Local 696.

726. "The New Militants." *Time*, 82 (August 16, 1963), 45.
The last year of Carl Megel's administration.

727. "New Wisconsin Bargaining Law for Teachers." *American Teacher*, 8 (March, 1962), 1–2.
The State Employment Relations Board schedules elections for teachers.

728. "New York City Wins Salary Raise, Bargaining Election." *American Teacher*, 7 (September, 1960), 2.
Success doubles the UFT membership.

729. "No Time to Strike, Keppel Tells AFT." *American School and University*, 38 (October, 1965), 68.

Contrast of views of the US Commissioner of Education and Charles Cogen.

730. Nolte, M. Chester. "Is the Board an 'Employer' under State's Labor Relations Law?" *American School Board Journal*, 151 (September, 1965), 9–10. Condensed in *Education Digest*, 31 (January, 1966), 34–35.

Ruling of the Kansas Supreme Court relating to collective bargaining laws and school boards.

731. Oakes, Russell C. "Should Teachers Strike? An Unanswered Question." *Journal of Educational Sociology*, 33 (March, 1960), 339–344.

Surveys teachers' union history and argues for a clear decision on the legality of strikes.

732. Perry, Charles R. "School Board–Staff Negotiations." *Teachers College Journal*, 37 (December, 1965), 103–109.

A comparison of the collective bargaining methods of the AFT and the NEA.

733. "Philadelphia, 3, Wins Election." *American Teacher*, 11 (March, 1965), 1–2.

The local wins by a vote larger than its official membership.

734. Porter, Robert G. "Collective Bargaining for Teachers." *American Teacher*, 45 (February, 1961), 9–10+.

Collective bargaining definitions, procedures, and the resulting legal questions.

735. Radke, Mrs. Fred A. "Real Significance of Collective Bargaining for Teachers." *Labor Law Journal*, 15 (December, 1964), 795–801.

A National School Boards Association official explains the group's opposition to collective bargaining.

736. "Referendum on AFT Federal Aid Policy Submitted to Members by Executive Council." *American Teacher*, 11 (March 15, 1965), 1–4.

A special referendum issue, together with the text of the proposed legislation, with arguments for and against passage.

737. Reuter, George S. "Salaries and Fringe Benefits." *American Teacher*, 45 (February, 1961), 11–12.
A guide to a bargaining position.

738. Reuther, Walter P. "The New Role of the Teacher in Society." *American Teacher*, 47 (December, 1962), 5–6+.
Projects the place of the AFT in the wide labor and social reform movements.

739. _____. "The Road to a Bright Tomorrow for Teachers." *American Teacher*, 48 (April, 1964), 5–6+.
AFL-CIO Industrial Union Department support for the AFT.

740. Rhodes, Eric F. "It's Time to Set the Record Straight." *Michigan Education Journal*, 38 (April 1, 1961), 543–544+.
Calls the UFT strike of 1961 a failure.

741. _____. "The New York City Teacher Election." *NEA Journal*, 51 (February, 1962), 21–22.
On the UFT representation victory in 1961.

742. Riordan, Mary Ellen. "Operation Bandwagon in Detroit." *American Teacher*, 48 (October, 1963), 15–16.
Progress toward collective bargaining.

743. Rudoff, Harvey and Gary Hellman. "Should Teachers Join a Union?" *Parents Magazine*, 40 (October, 1965), 60–61+.
Authors take opposing sides on union issues.

744. Scanlon, John. "Strikes, Sanctions, and the Schools." *Saturday Review*, 46 (October 19, 1963), 51–55, 71–74.
A general survey of positions taken by the AFT and the NEA in the early 1960s.

745. Schoemann, Peter T. "The Right of Teachers to Organize." *American Federationist*, 70 (March, 1963), 23–24. See also Margaret E. Jenkins, "America's Teachers, Their Rights and Responsibilities." *PTA Magazine*, 57 (September, 1962), 2–3.
Refutes charges of irresponsibility.

746. Seitz, Reynolds C. "School Boards and Teacher Unions." *American School Board Journal*, 141 (August, 1960), 11–13+.
   Citing a 1951 Connecticut Supreme Court decision allowing unions for public employees, author supports collective bargaining on teacher salaries.

747. Selden, David. "Class Size and the New York Contract." *Phi Delta Kappan*, 45 (March, 1964), 283–287.
   The 1963 UFT contract sets a precedent.

748. _____. "Needed: More Teacher Strikes." *Saturday Review*, 48 (May 15, 1965), 75.
   Strikes can be a valuable asset in gaining benefits.

749. _____. "Why Teachers Need the AFL-CIO." *American Teacher*, 49 (April, 1965), 9–10.
   Reminds members of labor backing for collective bargaining legislation, federal aid to education.

750. Shanker, Albert. "Local 2 Bargaining Agent." *American Teacher*, 8 (January, 1962), 1–2.
   A 2-to-1 victory for the UFT.

751. _____. "N.Y.C. Wins More Money." *American Teacher*, 8 (May, 1962), 1–2.
   One-day strike by the UFT.

752. Shoben, Edward Joseph, Jr. "When Teachers Strike." *Teachers College Record*, 65 (November, 1963), 164–167.
   The legality and morality of the 1963 UFT strike.

753. Smith, Charles O. "The Gary Victory." *American Teacher*, 48 (October, 1963), 9–10+.
   Local 4 becomes the bargaining agent for Gary teachers.

754. Smith, Fred M. "The Teachers Union *vs.* the Professional Association." *School and Society*, 90 (December 15, 1962), 439–440.
   Suggests that AFT success in New York City could lead to "fundamental change" in teachers' organizations.

755. Spero, Sterling D. "The New York Teachers' Strike." *Good Government*, 79 (September, 1962), 37-39.
     Argues for legalized collective bargaining; compares the early UFT strikes to "French demonstrations."

756. Starie, John H. and Jack Spatafora. "Union or Professional Membership: A Matter of Philosophy and Program." *NEA Journal*, 51 (March, 1962), 80-81.
     The NEA position, "independence" *vs.* unionization.

757. Stoneking, Wayne A. "What Are the Specifics of Professionalism?" *Illinois Education*, 51 (October, 1962), 58-59+.
     "Affiliation with labor violates the principle of devotion to calling."

758. Story, Harold W. "Collective Bargaining with Teachers under Wisconsin Law." *Theory into Practice*, 4 (April, 1965), 61-65. See also Harold W. Story, "Collective Bargaining under Wisconsin Law," *Teachers College Journal*, 37 (December, 1965), 110-115.
     State legislation of 1959 and 1961.

759. Strickland, Jack F. "The 49th Convention of the Federation of Teachers." *Monthly Labor Review*, 88 (October, 1965), 1204-1205.
     A report from Los Angeles, "the AFT appears to be sustaining its momentum."

760. "Teacher Union Leaders in Selma March." *American Teacher*, 11 (May, 1965), 2. See also *American Teacher*, 11 (June, 1965), 16.
     Charles Cogen, Albert Shanker, and others join Martin Luther King. Shanker later answers criticism of their participation.

761. "Teacher Union Promises More Militant Drive." *American School and University*, 37 (October, 1964), 21.
     On the election of Charles Cogen as AFT president.

762. "Teacher's Choice." *Economist,* 201 (December 23, 1961), 1218.
    A British report on the formation of the UFT.

763. "Teachers' Right to Strike." *School and Society,* 92 (March 7, 1964), 93–94.
    Editorial comment on the American Civil Liberties Union's support for the right to strike.

764. "Teachers' Strikes." *American School Board Journal,* 141 (December, 1960), 34.
    Editorial condemns the one-day strike by the UFT in November, 1960.

765. "Texas Teachers at Alamo." *American Teacher,* 6 (March, 1960), 1–2.
    Union struggles in Houston and San Antonio.

766. "Union Blocking Tactics Harass Teachers." *Michigan Education Journal,* 43 (December, 1965), 3–4.
    An NEA view of union rivalry in Michigan.

767. "Union Label." *Newsweek,* 60 (September 3, 1962), 51.
    A brief report on the 1962 convention.

768. "Unions Cash in on Teachers' Strikes." *Business Week,* 78 (September 1, 1962), 78.
    A brief report on the 1962 convention.

769. "United Action '64–'65, Key to Victory." *American Teacher,* 11 (June, 1965), 7–10.
    The year reviewed with text and pictures.

770. Wagner, Geoffrey. "Local 1460." *University Quarterly,* 19 (December, 1964), 78–80.
    A British report on the UFCT.

771. West, Allan M. "Professional Negotiations or Collective Bargaining?" *National Elementary Principal,* 42 (February, 1963), 20–25.

Anti-AFT views inspired by news of the union's organization drive with AFL-CIO support.

772. "When Teachers Organize." *Monthly Labor Review,* 87 (November, 1964), 1295–1296.
Comparison of the bargaining methods of the AFT and the NEA.

773. Wildman, Wesley A. "Collective Action by Public School Teachers." *Industrial and Labor Relations Review,* 18 (October, 1964), 3–19.
Review and definition, with annotations, of various aspects of collective action by the AFT and the NEA.

774. _____. "Legal Aspects of Teacher Collective Action." *Theory into Practice,* 4 (April, 1965), 55–60.
Summary of the union's legal position in 1965.

775. Winick, Charles. "When Teachers Strike." *Teachers College Record,* 64 (April, 1963), 593–604.
Survey of teacher and parent views on the 1960 UFT strike.

776. Wirth, Richard M. "Let's Be Sane About the Union." *Michigan Education Journal,* 40 (October, 1962), 204–205.
Maintains that the NEA is as effective as the AFT without worker-management "class struggle."

777. Wyatt, Robert A. and Robert Thornberry. "Viewpoints on Negotiations Vary." *Teachers College Journal,* 37 (December, 1965), 102+.
Contrasting the views of Thornberry of the Indiana Federation of Teachers, and Wyatt, a former president of the NEA.

778. Zerucha, Steve. "AFT Teachers Agent in 4th Major City." *American Teacher,* 11 (September, 1964), 1–2.
Victory over the NEA in Cleveland.

779. Ackerlund, George C. and David E. Elder. "Public Education and the Teachers Union." *Illinois Education*, 55 (December, 1966), 169–172.
An Illinois Education Association official argues that unionization violates the impartiality of schools.

780. "AFT Adopts Decentralization Policy." *American Teacher*, 53 (September, 1968), 4.
"Teachers and community must plan together."

781. "AFT and the Colleges." *American Teacher*, 12 (May, 1966), 8–9.
Testimony from St. John's, San Diego State, and Wayne State universities.

782. "AFT Gets a Black Caucus." *American Teacher*, 54 (October, 1969), 15–16.
Nineteen-sixty-nine convention developments designed to promote black participation in the union.

783. "AFT Maintains Strong Lead in Bargaining Agent Elections." *American Teacher*, 51 (January, 1967), 6.
Survey of elections in twelve states.

784. "AFT Maps Teacher Power Drive." *American Teacher*, 53 (September, 1968), 3+.
Early program of the David Selden administration.

785. "AFT Members Will Vote on Vietnam." *American Teacher*, 52 (April, 1968), 10–12; (June, 1968), 11+.
Confirms a continued neutral position on the war.

786. "AFT–NEA Units Merge in Flint." *American Teacher*, 54 (November, 1969), 5.
Historic local merger in Michigan.

787. "AFT's New York City Local Responds to the Bundy Report." *American Teacher*, 52 (January, 1968), 14.

The initial UFT objections to the Bundy report, with counterproposals.

788. Alsworth, Philip L. and Roger R. Woock. "Ocean Hill-Brownsville: Urban Conflict and the Schools." *Urban Education*, 4 (April, 1969), 25-40.
Predicts that 1968 would be the beginning of the decentralization movement.

789. Andreasen, Haakon L. "Teacher Unionism: Personal Data Affecting Membership." *Phi Delta Kappan*, 50 (November, 1968), 177.
Poll results indicate that AFT members are better educated and more dedicated than their NEA counterparts.

790. Andrews, J. Edward, Jr. "AFT and NEA: What Are the Issues?" *Educational Leadership*, 26 (March, 1969), 535-538.
A survey of issues common to both organizations.

791. Armstrong, Richard. "McGeorge Bundy Confronts the Teachers." *New York Times Magazine*, (April 20, 1969), 25-27+.
Role of the Ford Foundation and its president in the New York school decentralization plans of 1968.

792. "Association, Union Tactics Contrasted in Dayton Election." *Ohio Schools*, 47 (March 28, 1969), 7-8.
Victory of an NEA affiliate over its AFT rival in Dayton, Ohio.

793. "Bargaining Goal: 20 Pupils, 20 Hours." *American Teacher*, 54 (September, 1969), 25-26.
Survey of the union stand on working conditions.

794. Batchelder, Richard. "Unionism *versus* Professionalism." *Ohio Schools*, 44 (March, 1966), 24-29. Condensed in *NEA Journal*, 55 (April, 1966), 18-20.
Argues that the AFT threatens teacher independence and the freedom to teach.

795. Beitz, Joanne, "Thinking about Professional Organizations: NEA or AFT." *Contemporary Education*, 41 (November, 1969), 82-85.

Claims that AFT members are, in general, older, more financially pressed, but better educated than NEA counterparts.

796. Belasco, James A., et al. "A Case Analysis of Negotiation Behavior in an Urban School System." *Education and Urban Society*, 2 (November, 1969), 22–39.
A study of the 1967 UFT strike. Taylor Law (1967) is blamed for increased work stoppages.

797. Berry, John N., III. "Join the Picket Line!" *Library Journal*, 91 (April 1, 1966), 1782–1787.
Librarians participate in the 1966 UFCT strike at St. John's University.

798. Berube, Maurice R. "Scarsdale Yes, Harlem No: Community Control of Schools." *Commonweal*, 88 (June 21, 1968), 399–400. Reply by Patrick O'Grady, with rejoinder, *Commonweal*, 88 (August 9, 1968), 515+.
Criticism of the UFT in the Ocean Hill-Brownsville dispute.

799. _____. "Strike at St. John's: Why the Professors Picket." *Nation*, 202 (February 14, 1966), 172–174.
The strike by the United Federation of College Teachers, an AFT local at St. John's University, has given new impetus to college unionism.

800. "The Big Push in Federal School Aid—Loaf of Bread or Bag of Crumbs?" *American Teacher*, 51 (September, 1966), 17–18.
AFT leaders criticize the lack of a realistic approach to school aid.

801. "Blacklisting the Books." *Michigan Education Journal*, 43 (January, 1966), 20.
Charges that the AFT seeks to ban books expressing anti-union views or printed by non-union shops.

802. Blanke, Virgil E. "Teachers in Search of Power." *Educational Forum*, 30 (January, 1966), 231–238. Condensed in *American School Board Journal*, 151 (November, 1965), 7–9.

Emphasizes the AFT–NEA rivalry as a reason for increasing collective activity by teachers.

803. Bleeker, Ted. "Decentralization Battle Continues in New York." *American Teacher,* 53 (September, 1968), 11+. See also "Most Crippling Teacher Strike Ever: N.Y. Teachers Battle for Due Process," *American Teacher,* 53 (October, 1968), 4–5; "Press Fight for Teacher Rights: Agreement Sabotaged, Teachers Strike Again," *American Teacher,* 53 (November, 1968), 6; "Agreement Ends Third Strike: Back to School for NYC Teachers, Pupils," *American Teacher,* 53 (December, 1968), 6–7.

    A documentation of NYC teachers' strike.

804. Brann, James. "Unionizing the Academics." *New Republic,* 156 (February 25, 1967), 10–11.

    A report concentrating on AFT organizing in California.

805. Braun, Robert J. "Anatomy of a Strike: What Really Happened in Woodbridge." *School Management,* 11 (May, 1967), 76–82+.

    An analysis of the bitter New Jersey teacher strike, 1966–1967.

806. Brown, George W. "Teacher Power Techniques: Serious New Problems." *American School Board Journal,* 152 (February, 1966), 11–13.

    Argues that teacher militancy is "fed and fertilized by competition between the NEA and the AFT."

807. Brown, Ralph S., Jr. "Collective Bargaining in Higher Education." *Michigan Law Review,* 67 (March, 1969), 1067–1082.

    Compares positions and records of the AFT and the AAUP in faculty representation.

808. Carlton, Patrick W. "Labor Psychology and Industrial Planning." *Educational Leadership,* 25 (February, 1968), 423–425+.

Views collective bargaining as "a productive vehicle for improving educational planning."

809. Channin, Robert. "A Candid Look at the Profession." *Pennsylvania School Journal*, 116 (March. 1968), 368–370+.
Maintains that labor affiliation violates the "unity of the profession."

810. Cogen, Charles. "Rebuilding American Education." *American Teacher*, 52 (September, 1967), 11–15.
AFT president calls for a national master plan for education.

811. _____. "Teacher Militancy: Bridge to AFT–NEA Unity?" *American Teacher*, 52 (March, 1968), 2.
Urges the AFT to honor NEA strikes.

812. _____. "What Teachers Really Want from School Boards." *American School Board Journal*, 156 (February, 1969), 9–11.
Contends board–teacher conflicts are inherent and proper.

813. Cogen, Charles and David Selden. "American Federation of Teachers' Position Paper." *School and Society*, 95 (February 4, 1967), 87–91.
Statement issued at the Conference for Educating the Disadvantaged, Washington, D.C., 1966.

814. Cole, Stephen. "Teachers' Strike: A Study of the Conversion of Predisposition into Action." *American Journal of Sociology*, 74 (March, 1969), 506–520.
A study of personal motivations of participants in the UFT strike of 1962.

815. _____. "Unionization of Teachers: Determinants of Rank-and-File Support." *Sociology of Education*, 41 (Winter, 1968), 66–87.
A study of factors in the backgrounds of teachers ("non-teaching statuses") affecting attitudes toward union membership.

816. Collins, Harold W. and Norbert J. Nelson. "A Study of Teacher Morale: Union (AFT) Teachers *versus* Non-Union

(NEA) Teachers." *Journal of Educational Research,* 62 (September, 1968), 3–10.
Study indicates union membership improves the morale of male but not female teachers.

817. "Coming Rash of Teacher Strikes." *U.S. News and World Report,* 65 (September 2, 1968), 41–42.
Compares teacher strikes to an epidemic.

818. "Coming to Grips with Racism." *American Teacher,* 51 (January, 1967), 11–14. See also Ossie Davis, "The English Language Is My Enemy," *American Teacher,* 51 (April, 1967), 13+; "Racism in Education," *American Teacher,* 51 (May, 1967), 8–9+.
AFT Conference on Racism in Education held in Washington, D.C., December, 1966.

819. Cook, Alice H. "Union Structure in Municipal Collective Bargaining." *Monthly Labor Review,* 89 (June, 1966), 606–608.
Compares the UFT and the American Federation of State, County, and Municipal Employees.

820. Craft, James A. "Proportional Representation for Teacher Negotiations." *Industrial Relations,* 8 (May, 1969), 236–246.
The effect of the Winton Act (1965) on union organizing and representation in California.

821. Dashiell, Dick. "Teachers Revolt in Michigan." *Phi Delta Kappan,* 49 (September, 1967), 20–26.
Reports that Michigan teachers have more dignity under collective bargaining and tenure.

822. Davison, William E. "Decentralization Touches Off Power Struggle." *Michigan Education Journal,* 46 (November, 1968), 27–28.
Indicates that the NEA favors New York City school decentralization in opposition to the UFT's plan.

823. Day, James F. and William H. Fisher. "The Professor and

Collective Negotiations." *School and Society*, 95 (April 1, 1967), 226–229.

Predicts growth of AFT membership in college faculties and possible merger with the AAUP and the NEA.

824. "Desegregation in Northern Schools." *American Teacher*, 53 (December, 1969), 2–3.

Union policies in New York, Philadelphia, Detroit, and other cities.

825. Dewing, Rolland. "Is an NEA–AFT Merger Imminent?" *Peabody Journal of Education*, 47 (July, 1969), 43–47. Condensed in *Education Digest*, 35 (November, 1969), 35–37.

Blames the AFT's debts, factionalism, and urban school woes for the delay in merger plans.

826. _____. "Teacher Organizations and Desegregation." *Phi Delta Kappan*, 49 (January, 1968), 257–260. See also Albert Shanker, "The Real Meaning of the New York City Teachers' Strike." *Phi Delta Kappan*, 50 (April, 1969), 434–441.

Dissatisfaction of some black teachers with the AFT despite the union's civil rights record.

827. Doherty, Robert E. "Determination of Bargaining Units and Election Procedures in Public School Teacher Representation Elections." *Industrial and Labor Relations Review*, 19 (July, 1966), 573–595.

Compares bargaining unit elections of districts won by the AFT *vs.* those won by the NEA.

828. _____. "The Impact of Teacher Organizations upon Setting School Negotiation Policies." *Clearing House*, 40 (May, 1966), 515–524.

Asks for moderation on both sides in collective bargaining.

829. "$831 More for Union Teachers." *American Teacher*, 12 (February, 1966), 1–2.

The comparison of average US teacher salaries, 1965–1966, demonstrates AFT effectiveness.

830. Elam, Stanley M. "NEA–AFT Merger—And Related Matters." *Phi Delta Kappan*, 47 (February, 1966), 285–286.

Editorial claims merger would be unworkable without further preparation and substantial membership support.

831. Elsila, David. "AFT Helps Fill a Gap for South's Educationally Starved." *American Teacher*, 51 (September, 1966), 11–14.
An account of the Mississippi Freedom School movement.

832. _____. "Teachers Join the Fight to Keep the Schools Free." *American Teacher*, 52 (December, 1967), 15.
Teacher attempts to prevent the ban of controversial books in schools.

833. "Enforcing One Injunction, at Least." *Time*, 90 (October 13, 1967), 58.
The New York Supreme Court rules against the UFT by enforcing the no-strike Taylor Law.

834. Epperson, David C. "Teacher Heresy in the Union Movement." *Educational Forum*, 30 (May, 1966), 433–438.
Charges that the views of a union leader hinder attempts toward quality education for children of working-class parents.

835. "An Essential Difference." *Pennsylvania School Journal*, 117 (October, 1968), 85.
Editorial contends that union membership demeans teachers by grouping them with "ordinary factory workers."

836. "Ferment on the Campus: The St. John's Story." *American Teacher*, 12 (January, 1966), 9, 12.
A bitter strike at the largest Catholic university renews debate about the union's position with college faculties.

837. "The First Cooperative Conference." *Negro History Bulletin*, 30 (April, 1967), 20.
A report on the first conference on "Correcting America's Image of the Past" co-sponsored by the AFT.

838. " 'First Lady' of the Convention." *American Teacher*, 54 (October, 1969), 9–10.
Mary McGough, who was a delegate to over forty conventions, comments on union history.

125

839. Flynn, Ralph J. "When the Votes are Counted." *NEA Journal*, 56 (May, 1967), 48+.
Reassures NEA members that the AFT will not dominate the teaching profession.

840. Fondy, Albert. "A Logical Defense of Teacher Strikes." *Changing Education*, 4 (Winter, 1969), 27.
On the illogic and inequity of anti-strike legislation.

841. Freiser, Leonard H. "The Bloomers of My Aunt, or, Does the Union Suit?" *Library Journal*, 93 (December 15, 1968), 4629. Reply, *Library Journal*, 94 (February 1, 1969), 475.
A New York library executive finds UFT affiliation "disgusting."

842. Galamison, Milton A. "The Ocean Hill-Brownsville Dispute: Urban School Crisis in Microcosm." *Christianity and Crisis*, 28 (October 14, 1968), 239–241.
Criticizes an "unholy alliance" between the UFT and the New York School Board.

843. Garbarino, Joseph W. "Professional Negotiations in Education." *Industrial Relations*, 7 (February, 1968), 93–106.
"Unions will act like unions" despite professional rhetoric.

844. Gittell, Marilyn R. "Teacher Power and Its Implications for Urban Education." *Theory into Practice*, 7 (April, 1968), 80–82.
Credits the UFT alone among urban locals with major involvement in issues other than salary questions.

845. Glass, Ronald W. "Work Stoppages and Teachers: History and Prospect." *Monthly Labor Review*, 90 (August, 1967), 43–46.
A study of 1966 teacher strikes most of which involved the AFT.

846. Goss, Charles E. "Before the AFT: The Texas Experience." *Changing Education*, 1 (Summer, 1966), 6–9.
San Antonio, Texas, 1902–1910, is the first teachers' organization to affiliate with the AFL.

126

847. Gotesky, Rubin. "Charter of Academic Rights and Governance." *Educational Forum*, 32 (November, 1967), 9–18.
Advocates a legal charter defining the rights of college faculty unions.

848. Hale, Hattie. "Florida's Bad Dream." *American Teacher*, 52 (April, 1968), 4–5. See also "2000 Florida Teachers Leave NEA to Join Union," *American Teacher*, 52 (May, 1968), 3.
A disastrous NEA strike in Florida.

849. Hannan, Cecil J. "Professional Negotiation Means an Independent Profession with a Strong Voice." *Kentucky School Journal*, 45 (November, 1966), 24–25.
Charges that AFT membership entails a loss of "professional independence" to labor.

850. Hanson, Earl H. "Should the NEA and the AFT Unite?" *Education*, 87 (December, 1966), 253.
A former school superintendent calls labor affiliation "improper."

851. Hazard, William R. "Collective Bargaining in Education: The Anatomy of a Problem." *Labor Law Journal*, 18 (July, 1967), 412–419.
Stresses how much the NEA has imitated the AFT.

852. _____. "Semantic Gymnastics?" *American School Board Journal*, 155 (October, 1967), 14–20.
Argues that the NEA has come to duplicate the AFT in all major respects.

853. Heim, Peggy. "Growing Tensions in Academic Administration." *North Central Association Quarterly*, 42 (Winter, 1968), 244–251.
College faculty discontent as reflected in the programs of the AFT and AAUP.

854. Hentoff, Nat. "Ocean Hill-Brownsville and the Future of Community Control." *Civil Liberties*, 260 (February, 1969), 1–5.

Praises the flexibility of the Washington (D.C.) Teachers' Union in contrast to the "rigidly defensive" UFT.

855. Hixson, Richard. "Four Associations Look to the Junior College: American Federation of Teachers." *Junior College Journal*, 39 (December, 1968), 10+.
Urges greater cooperation among local federations of junior college faculty.

856. Holzman, Seymour. "AFT: Action on the Picket Line." *Senior Scholastic*, (Teacher Supplement), 95 (September 29, 1969), 1–2.
A report on the 1969 convention.

857. _____. "AFT Arms for Merger with NEA." *Senior Scholastic*, (Teacher Supplement), 93 (September 27, 1968), 6.
A review of the AFT positions on merger, decentralization, and membership for paraprofessionals.

858. Hopkins, Maurice D. "Development of a Collective Bargaining Relationship." *Bulletin of the National Association of Secondary School Principals*, 52 (May, 1968), 93–104.
A New York school administrator admits "unionization is here to stay" and advises his colleagues to cooperate.

859. Horchler, Richard. "The Time Bomb in Catholic Education." *Look*, 30 (April 5, 1966), 23–25.
On the UFCT strike at St. John's University in 1966.

860. Howat, John J. "The Nature of Teacher Power and Teacher Attitudes Toward Certain Aspects of This Power." *Theory into Practice*, 7 (April, 1968), 51 56.
Teacher power is legitimate and strikes for recognition are justified.

861. Howe, Ray. "Teachers Must Lead in Staff Integration." *American Teacher*, 12 (January, 1966), 5+.
Admits the issue raises problems regarding seniority.

862. "Interview with Albert Shanker." *Urban Review*, 3 (November, 1968), 18–27.

Shanker's views on "performance contractors," account-ability, tenure, and such matters.

863. "Jailing of Shanker Spurs Nationwide Effort to Fight Antistrike Legislation." *American Teacher*, 52 (January, 1968), 1+.
Albert Shanker serves fifteen days for contempt of court.

864. Janssen, Peter. "The Union Response to Academic Mass Production." *Saturday Review*, 50 (October 21, 1967), 64–66+.
A survey of the AFT's "almost frantic growth."

865. Julian, Bernadette S. "The AFT in Caucus and Convention: New Style for 1967." *Monthly Labor Review*, 90 (November, 1967), 19–20.
A report on the 1967 convention.

866. Kaplan, Joel. "Can a Teachers Union Be Professional?" *Changing Education*, 1 (Summer, 1966), 36–46.
A history of the UFT's early years, emphasizing the commitment to more than salary increases.

867. Kemble, Eugenia. "Professional Employees and Unions." *American Teacher*, 52 (January, 1968), 17+.
On SPACE, the AFL-CIO's Council of Scientific, Professional, and Cultural Employees.

868. Keyserling, Leon. "A 10-Year Plan to Save the Schools." *American Teacher*, 53 (September, 1968), 12–13.
A noted economist's blueprint for reshaping the financial structure of our public school systems.

869. Kite, Robert H. "What We Do or What We Get." *Educational Forum*, 32 (March, 1968), 265–275.
Regards union membership "unprofessional."

870. Klaus, Ida. "The Evolution of a Collective Bargaining Relationship in Public Education: New York's Changing Seven-Year History." *Michigan Law Review*, 67 (March, 1969), 1033–1066.
Traces the development of UFT positions on collective

bargaining, salary and working conditions agreements, and the MES program, since 1962.

871. Landis, Elwood W. "Charges of Unfair Labor Practices: When Do They Block Teachers and When Do They Help Teachers?" *Michigan Education Journal*, 43 (February, 1966), 10–13.
Warns that the AFT could lead teachers into a "morass of litigation."

872. Larsen, C. M. " 'Collective Bargaining' Issues in the California State Colleges." *AAUP Bulletin*, 53 (June, 1967), 217–227.
Discusses an AFT attempt to become sole bargaining agent for the California state colleges in 1966.

873. Leo, John. "Black Anti-Semitism." *Commonweal*, 89 (February 14, 1969), 618–620.
Author charges that Albert Shanker "manipulated" fears of anti-Semitism to the advantage of the UFT.

874. Levine, Marvin J. "Higher Education and Collective Action: Will Professors Unionize?" *Journal of Higher Education*, 38 (May, 1967), 263–268.
Identifies AFT affiliates on college campuses as the most strike-prone.

875. Lieberman, Myron. "Implications of the Coming NEA–AFT Merger." *Phi Delta Kappan*, 50 (November, 1968), 139–144.
Concentrates on issues dividing the two groups.

876. Livingston, John C. "Collective Bargaining and Professionalism in Higher Education." *Education Record*, 48 (Winter, 1967), 79–88.
Collective bargaining is viewed as a response to problems resulting from a breakdown of authority.

877. Lloyd, John H. "AFT Wants New Standards." *Senior Scholastic* (Teacher Supplement), 91 (September 28, 1967), 2.
A report on the 1967 convention.

878. _____. "Washington Report." *Senior Scholastic* (Teacher Supplement), 89 (September 30, 1966), 8.
A report on the 1966 convention.

879. _____. "Washington Report." *Senior Scholastic* (Teacher Supplement), 91 (September 28, 1967), 20.
Predicts little likelihood of an AFT–NEA merger.

880. McHugh, William F. "Collective Negotiation in Public Higher Education." *College and University Business*, 47 (December, 1969), 41–44+.
On the effect of the Taylor Law (1967) on New York State faculty unions.

881. McLennan, Kenneth and Michael H. Moskow. "Teacher Strikes: Their Causes and Their Impact." *Management of Personnel Quarterly*, 7 (Fall, 1968), 20–23.
Advocates finding alternatives to, rather than legalization of, teacher strikes.

882. "Making 'Workers Education' Work." *American Teacher*, 51 (April, 1967), 7–8.
On Workers Education Local 189 (formerly of Brookwood Labor College).

883. Marmion, Harry A. "Unions and Higher Education." *Educational Record*, 49 (Winter, 1968), 41–48.
Argues for reforms to stave off unionization of college faculties.

884. Mayer, Martin. "The Full and Sometimes Very Surprising Story of Ocean Hill, the Teachers' Union, and the Teacher Strike of 1968." *New York Times Magazine*, 118 (February 2, 1969), 18–23.
A lengthy condensation of Mayer's book on New York's "worst disaster."

885. Meier, Deborah. "The New York Teachers' Strike." *Midstream*, 13 (December, 1967), 36–47.

131

Stresses the professional aims of the UFT strike of 1967; discusses charges of racism leveled against the local.

886. Mesirow, David. "The AFT's Role in the Thirties." *Changing Education*, 1 (Summer, 1966), 28–31, 51.
Views the fight for tenure and for academic freedom as the most important union issues of the thirties.

887. Morris, Frank. "Teachers and the Yellow-Dog Rule: The Seattle Story." *Changing Education*, 1 (Summer, 1966), 18–25.
A history of Local 200's fight for survival, 1927–1931.

888. Moskow, Michael H. "Representation among Teachers." *Monthly Labor Review*, 89 (July, 1966), 728–732.
Reviews AFT and NEA policies on exclusive *vs.* proportional systems of representation.

889. Moskow, Michael H. and Kenneth McLennan. "Teacher Strikes and Dispute Settlement Policy." *New York Law Forum*, 14 (Summer, 1968), 281–293.
Reviews the effects of New York State's Taylor Law.

890. Muir, Douglas. "The Strike as Professional Sanction: The Changing Attitude of the National Education Association." *Labor Law Journal*, 19 (October, 1968), 615–627.
"The AFT has acted as the spark to ignite the lethargic engine of the NEA."

891. Muir, J. D. "The Tough New Teacher." *American School Board Journal*, 156 (November, 1968), 9–14.
A history of the NEA in the 1960s discusses AFT and AFL-CIO influence.

892. "NEA/AFT Merger: Five Years Away, Schoolmen Say." *Nation's Schools*, 81 (June, 1968), 60.
A poll of school administrators reveals strong opposition to a merger.

893. "NEA Officials Explain Refusal to Talk Merger with AFT." *Phi Delta Kappan*, 50 (February, 1969), 319.
Mergers on the local level are regarded as better than "from the top down."

894. Neirynck, Robert W. "Teacher Strikes—A New Militancy." *Notre Dame Lawyer*, 43 (February, 1968), 367–388. See also *Labor Law Journal*, 19 (May, 1968), 292–312.

A survey of key strike cases recommends a limited right to strike for teachers.

895. "New Targets for Teachers' Union." *U.S. News and World Report*, 60 (January 31, 1966), 80.

A report on the organizing drive in both school districts and colleges.

896. "New York Library Teachers Win Arbitration Nod." *Library Journal*, 94 (May 15, 1969), 1934. See also Sylvia Mendlow, "Teachers of Library Unite!" *Library Journal*, 94 (July, 1969), 2537–2538.

On a ruling limiting the number of teaching periods assigned to library teachers.

897. Nolte, M. Chester. "How Not to Pay Damages: Don't Penalize Teachers for Unionism." *American School Board Journal*, 156 (April, 1969), 8+.

Warns school boards that recent court decisions favor teacher union activity regardless of state laws.

898. ———. "Teachers Seek Greater Independence through Legislative Channels." *American School Board Journal*, 152 (March, 1966), 7–9.

Discusses recent legislative steps favoring teacher unions.

899. Penski, Robert J. "John Dewey and the Nature of Democracy: The Case of Local 5, American Federation of Teachers." *Industrial and Labor Relations Forum*, 5 (November, 1968), 271–306.

A sympathetic account of the Local 5 radical faction and an attack upon Linville as "underhanded, sly, and outright undemocratic."

900. Peterson, Leroy. "Legal Status of Teacher Personnel." *Review of Educational Research*, 37 (June, 1967), 296–299.

Survey of literature on the subject, 1963–1966.

901. Porter, Robert G. and Charles Miller. "Landmark Cases—I:

Marvin Pickering's Fight for Equal Rights." *American Teacher*, 53 (January, 1969), 11. See also Robert G. Porter and Charles Miller, "Landmark Cases—II: Battling 'Loyalty' Oaths: Saga of the Elfbrandts," *American Teacher*, (February, 1969), 19.

One of a series of articles on union defense of individual members.

902. Potts, Georgina R. "A Summer School Short Course in Teacher Negotiations." *Monthly Labor Review*, 89 (August, 1966), 847–850.

Tactics and theory as discussed at the National Institute of Collective Negotiation in Public Education, University of Pennsylvania, 1966.

903. "Proposals to Change the AFT Constitution." *American Teacher*, 53 (April, 1969), 14.

On strike insurance, membership restrictions, and other such matters.

904. "Pursuit of Power." *Time*, 90 (September 22, 1967), 43–44.

A report concentrating on the UFT strike of 1967.

905. "Questions and Answer about QuEST." *American Teacher*, 53 (October, 1968), 18–19; 53 (March, 1969), 13+; 53 (April, 1969), 13.

An interview with AFT research director Robert Bhaerman about the "Quality Education Standards in Teaching" program.

906. "Racism." *American Teacher*, 52 (May, 1968), 8+.

Local AFT programs against racial bias in education.

907. Raskin, A. H. "He Leads His Teachers Up the Down Staircase." *New York Times Magazine*, (September 3, 1967), 4–5+.

A favorable report on Albert Shanker's leadership of the UFT.

908. Reese, Arthur. "Freedom Schools: 1965 and 1966." *American Teacher*, 12 (February, 1966), 5–6+; (April, 1966), 7.

AFT support of programs for civil rights groups in Alabama, Florida, and Mississippi.

909. "Resolutions Provoke Debates on Student Rights, Other Issues." *American Teacher*, 54 (October, 1969), 11–14.
Student collective bargaining, honoring of picket lines.

910. Riesel, Victor. "Blackboard Power, Name of the Game." *Michigan Education Journal*, 54 (November, 1967), 1.
NEA reaction to AFT militancy.

911. Rinehart, Blanche. "Mr. Gompers and the Teachers." *Changing Education*, 1 (Summer, 1966), 12–17.
Discusses the influence of the AFL president on the founding of the AFT, 1913–1918.

912. Robinson, Donald W. "Teacher Militancy around the Nation." *Phi Delta Kappan*, 49 (June, 1968), 554.
The differences in teacher strikes among the states; cites predictions for the future.

913. Rosenthal, Alan. "New Voices in Public Education." *Teachers College Record*, 68 (October, 1966), 13–20.
Discusses efforts by the UFT toward a more decisive voice in educational policy-making.

914. _____. "The Strength of Teacher Organizations: Factors Influencing Membership in Two Large Cities." *Sociology of Education*, 39 (Fall, 1966), 359–380.
A study of the UFT, the Boston Teachers Union, and the Boston Teachers Alliance.

915. Ross, Anne M. "The AFT: Local Control, Money and Merger." *Monthly Labor Review*, 91 (November, 1968), 18–20.
Three chief issues of the 1968 convention.

916. "St. John's Congress Postponed till May: Library School Boycott by UFCT Continues." *Library Journal*, 92 (February 1, 1967), 517+.
Effect of the strike at St. John's University on librarians.

917. "St. John's—Four Years Later." *American Teacher*, 54 (December, 1969), 8–9.
An account of unsuccessful negotiations at St. John's University.

918. "St. John's U. Firings Go to Arbitration." *American Teacher*, 52 (September, 1967), 1+.
Continued conflict at St. John's described.

919. Schnaufer, Pete. "Collective Bargaining Contracts." *American Teacher*, 51 (March, 1967), 9–16.
An analysis and comparison of AFT and NEA contracts.

920. "The Schools of the 70's: Where Will You Fit In?" *American Teacher*, 54 (September, 1969), 1–19.
Projections on organization, salaries, working conditions.

921. Schwager, Sidney. "MES: Real Hope for the Ghettos." *American Teacher*, 52 (December, 1967), 9–12; *American Teacher*, 53 (April, 1969), 7.
Account of the "More Effective Schools" Program in New York City. Articles on MES programs in various cities appear in subsequent issues.

922. Selden, David. "Parents' Role as AFT Sees It." *Senior Scholastic* (Teacher Supplement), 93 (November 1, 1968), 2–14.
Believes that "there should be no conflict between parents and teachers."

923. _____. "School Decentralization: A Positive Approach." *Teachers College Record*, 71 (September, 1969), 85–92.
Reasons that "moderate" decentralization could alleviate urban racial polarization without pitting teachers against parents.

924. _____. "Strikes, Sanctions, or Surrender?" *Childhood Education*, 45 (April, 1969), 445–447.
Affirms that the AFT goal is "good faith collective bargaining."

925. _____. "Why the AFT Maintains Its AFL-CIO Affiliation." *Phi Delta Kappan*, 47 (February, 1966), 298–300. Condensed in *Education Digest*, 31 (April, 1966), 19–21.
Labor affiliation is an expression of the AFT's commitment to social reform.

926. _____. "Work Stoppages and Teachers' Rights." *American Teacher*, 51 (March, 1967), 7.
    An AFT official insists upon the right to strike.

927. Scher, Richard K. "Decentralization and the New York State Legislature." *Urban Review*, 4 (September, 1969), 13–19.
    Discusses a 1968 New York State bill limiting school decentralization; credits the UFT with "tremendous leverage" in Albany.

928. Schmidt, Charles T., Jr. "Representation of Classroom Teachers." *Monthly Labor Review*, 91 (July, 1968), 27–36.
    Two case studies, Detroit and Grand Rapids, Michigan, are analyzed in the selection of bargaining representatives.

929. Shanker, Albert. "The Real Meaning of the New York Teachers Strike." *Phi Delta Kappan*, 50 (April, 1969), 434–441.
    Affirms a continued fight for the principles of integration and racial equality.

930. _____. "Schools and the Union." *New Republic*, 161 (November 15, 1969), 26–28+.
    Discusses the cooperation of the UFT and minority group leaders supporting the passage of the 1969 New York school decentralization law.

931. _____. "What's Wrong with Compensatory Education." *Saturday Review*, 52 (January 11, 1969), 56+.
    "Before we accept the slogan that 'money is not the answer' [to urban school problems] we ought to try the money approach just once."

932. Shanker, Albert, et al. "A Citizens' Review Board for Teachers?" *American Teacher*, 51 (December, 1966), 8–10.
    The UFT president's views contrast with those of the head of a parents' group and an ACLU director.

933. "Should NEA or AFT Membership Be Compulsory?" *Instructor*, 79 (December, 1969), 29.
    From a random sample of 100 subscribers, the majority disapprove of the agency shop.

934. "Should the AFT Relocate to Washington, D.C.?" *American Teacher*, 51 (April, 1967), 10–12+. See also "Referendum on Washington Move Passes," *American Teacher*, 51 (June, 1967), 3+.
    Arguments pro and con.

935. "A Shrewd Union Leader Takes His Teachers Out." *Life*, 63 (September 22, 1967), 32–35.
    A short pictorial report of the 1967 UFT strike.

936. Sigel, Efrem. "Memoir of a Non-Striking Teacher." *New Leader*, 52 (January 20, 1969), 11–14.
    Why one teacher crossed the 1968 UFT picket lines.

937. Slominsky, David T. "The Agreement and Some Implications for the New York City Elementary School Principal." *National Elementary Principal*, 46 (February, 1967), 35–37.
    A New York principal reviews the effects of the 1965 UFT contract.

938. Star, Jack. "Our Angry Teachers." *Look*, 32 (September 3, 1968), 64–66+.
    Emphasizes how the NEA copied AFT tactics.

939. Stern, Sol. " 'Scab' Teachers." *Ramparts*, 7 (November 17, 1968), 17–25.
    Criticism of the UFT in the Ocean Hill-Brownsville dispute.

940. Stratton, Myra. "Sister Scabs in the Suburbs." *Commonweal*, 88 (May 17, 1968), 255–256; (July 26, 1968), 482.
    On strikes by the Archdiocesan Teachers Federation, Local 1700, Chicago.

941. "Strike Cripples San Francisco State." *American Teacher*, 53 (February, 1969), 3+; (March, 1969), 3.
    A faculty strike is complicated by serious student unrest.

942. "Student Powers, Student Rights: The Federation's Views." *American Teacher*, 53 (April, 1969), 10.
    Favors democratic student unions and full civil liberties for students.

943. Swenson, Norman G. and Leon Novar. "Chicago City

College Teachers Strike." *Junior College Journal*, 37 (March, 1967), 19–22.

Two strikes (November, 1966 and January, 1967) force an administration to recognize the seriousness of teacher demands.

944. "Teacher Strikes: A Threat to Opening of Schools." *U.S. News and World Report*, 63 (September 4, 1967), 70–72.

A report on the nationwide patterns of teacher strikes in 1967.

945. "The Teacher Union Movement: Where It's At, Where It's Going." *American Teacher*, 52 (June, 1968), 2–10.

A survey of membership growth and union programs within the schools and without; plans for the future.

946. "Teacher Union's Rising Power—Fewer Strikes Ahead?" *U.S. News and World Report*, 67 (September 1, 1969), 56–57.

David Selden is quoted as predicting a lessening need to strike now that AFT strength is a proven factor.

947. "Teachers Get Militant." *Business Week*, August 17, 1968, p. 100.

Report on the 1968 convention.

948. "Teachers on Strike: What They Want Now." *U.S. News and World Report*, 65 (September 16, 1968), 83-84.

Brief report on the Ocean Hill-Brownsville dispute.

949. "Teachers Return to Classrooms with Bargaining Rights and Pay Hikes." *American Teacher*, 12 (April, 1966), 3.

Survey of union gains in New Orleans, Philadelphia, and suburban Chicago.

950. "Teachers Strike Hard." *Business Week*, September 16, 1967, pp. 43–44.

A review of AFT strikes in 1967 plus reaction of government and the NEA.

951. "Teachers Strikes Hit the Small Districts." *American Teacher*, 54 (October, 1969), 2–5.

Report of twenty-four strikes in the fall of 1969.

952. "Teachers Warn Boards: You Haven't Seen Anything Yet."
American School Board Journal, 156 (October, 1968), 28+.
A reaction to the 1968 convention and the promise of more
frequent strikes.

953. Thornton, Robert J. "Collective Negotiations for Teachers in
Illinois." *Illinois Business Review,* 26 (December, 1969), 6–8.
Unions raise salaries not only for their own members but for
unorganized teachers in neighboring districts as well.

954. "24 Illinois Teachers First to Donate to AFT's Teacher
Militancy Fund." *American Teacher,* 52 (March, 1968), 3; 52
(April, 1968), 1+.
A strike fund established after the jailing of Albert Shanker
and others.

955. "Two Candidates Seek Top Union Post." *American Teacher,*
12 (June, 1966), 6–7+. See also *American Teacher,* 51
(September, 1966), 3+, for report of Cogen's victory.
Charles Cogen *vs.* John Fewkes.

956. "The Union Grows: A Pictorial Record of 1965–66." *American Teacher,* 12 (June, 1966), 10–11.
Surveys developments in collective bargaining, strikes,
aid to education, and union services.

957. "Union Moves to Put S.F. Schools on Uphill Track."
American Teacher, 52 (January, 1968), 16+.
Programs of San Francisco Local 61.

958. "Union Protests Title II Practice." *Library Journal,* 92 (April
15, 1967), 1688+.
Reveals UFT dissatisfaction with the administration of
federal funds for library materials.

959. "Union's New 'Court of Last Resort.' " *American Teacher,*
52 (September, 1967), 9.
Reports the establishment of the Public Review Board.

960. "The Use and Misuse of Power." *Time,* 92 (October 25,
1968), 52+.

Author characterizes Albert Shanker as "a shrewd and sophisticated student of the uses of power."

961. "A 'Victory' for Teacher Power over Community Power in New York City?" *Phi Delta Kappan*, 50 (November, 1968), 138.
A report on the settlement of the 1968 UFT Ocean Hill-Brownsville strike.

962. "Washington and Baltimore Chart Plans for More Effective Schools." *American Teacher*, 12 (March, 1966), 8–9.
Focus on the abysmal school conditions in black neighborhoods.

963. "Washington Teachers Pick Union, 3–2, Right in NEA's Own Backyard." *American Teacher*, 51 (May, 1967), 3+.
Washington (D.C.) Local 6 is elected bargaining agent for teachers in the nation's capital.

964. Wasserman, Miriam and John Reimann. "Student Rebels *vs.* Student Defenders." *Urban Review*, 4 (October, 1969), 9–17.
Interviews with New York secondary school students are reported to reveal substantial hostility toward the UFT.

965. Wechsler, James A. "Civil War in New York." *Progressive*, 33 (January, 1969), 20–23.
Author criticizes the UFT for the "hate-drenched" strike in 1968.

966. "What Are Teachers Strikes Doing to Children?" *PTA Magazine*, 63 (November, 1968), 2–6, 36–37.
Cites the possible effects of strikes on children's attitudes toward teachers and the law.

967. "What Would Things Be Like If Teachers, Not Boards, Made Policy?" *American School Board Journal*, 157 (October, 1969), 32.
Reaction to issues discussed at the 1969 convention.

968. Whittier, C. Taylor. "Teacher Power as Viewed by the School Board and Superintendent." *Theory into Practice*, 7 (April, 1968), 76–79.

Observes that AFT rejection of the superintendent as a spokesman at least simplifies his role in negotiations.

969. Wildman, Wesley A. "Representing the Teachers' Interest: Conflict Issues in Negotiations." *Monthly Labor Review*, 89 (June, 1966), 617–623.
A paper on impasse resolution, with responses by Pete Schnaufer (AFT), Arnold W. Wolpert (NEA), and James G. Solberg (Menomonie, Wisconsin, school board).

970. _____. "What Prompts Greater Teacher Militancy?" *American School Board Journal*, 154 (March, 1967), 27–32.
A survey of principal bargaining issues nationwide contrasts the positions of the AFT and the NEA.

971. Wildman, Wesley A. and Charles R. Perry. "Group Conflict and School Organization." *Phi Delta Kappan*, 47 (January, 1966), 244–251.
"The AFT accepts as a given . . . significant conflict [between teachers and administrators]."

972. Wright, Melton. "Unions for Teachers?" *Virginia Journal of Education*, 60 (May, 1967), 15.
A stern warning to "reject the blandishments" of the AFT.

973. Young, Fred. "Collective Negotiation for North Carolina Teachers?" *Popular Government*, 34 (March, 1968), 1–8.
Despite "a non-union social climate," author predicts AFT organizing and collective bargaining demands.

974. Younger, George D. "Education Crisis: New York Style. Only the Beginning of an Ordeal." *Christianity and Crisis*, 28 (December 23, 1968), 312–317.
Criticism of the UFT as reactionary in the Ocean Hill-Brownsville dispute.

975. Zaner, Theodore. "Teacher Militancy: A Case Study of Contrasting Viewpoints." *Teachers College Record*, 70 (January, 1969), 321–330.
Strike by AFT teachers in Woodbridge Township, New Jersey, in 1967.

976. Zeluck, Stephen. "The UFT Strike: Will It Destroy the AFT?" *Phi Delta Kappan*, 50 (January, 1969), 250–254.

The president of New Rochelle (New York) Local 280 charges that the UFT betrayed its "noblest traditions" in its stand on decentralization in 1968.

977. _____. "What Chance for Educational Reform?" *Changing Education*, 3 (Winter, 1969), 39–41.

Suggestions for keeping alive the spirit of John Dewey in the modern AFT.

1970–1979

978. "Adult Educators Choose AFT in Wake of California Victories." *American Teacher*, 61 (March, 1977), 4.

The San Diego Community College Guild, AFT, Local 1931, becomes the exclusive bargaining agent for 1,200 adult educators.

979. "Affirmative Action Yes—Quotas No!" *American Teacher*, 62 (September, 1977), 12–13.

The 1977 AFT convention "calls for equal—not preferential treatment" in dealing with college admissions.

980. "AFT Conferences Set for May 10–12." *American Teacher*, 63 (April, 1979), 6, 17.

Previews the 1979 QuEST meeting and the AFT National Paraprofessional Conference.

981. "AFT Denounces Tuition Tax Credit Proposal." *American Teacher*, 62 (March, 1978), 1.

Shanker calls the tuition tax credit bill "the beginning of the end of public education in America."

982. "AFT Gears up to Meet Challenges." *American Teacher*, 62 (September, 1977), 9–11.

Reports on the sixty-first annual AFT convention.

983. "AFT in '72–'73: Days of Struggle, Year of Gains." *American Teacher*, 57 (June, 1973), 1A–12A.

   A summary of the year's events: unparalleled growth, reform programs, strikes.

984. "AFT Joins Other Unions in Pro-ERA Media Campaign." *American Teacher*, 61 (April, 1977), 22.

   Florida radio advertising is purchased.

985. "AFT-Labor Open Stop-Marland Drive." *American Teacher*, 55 (October, 1970), 3. See also David Selden, "Education under Siege," *American Teacher*, 55 (October, 1970), 7–10.

   On protests against Nixon's Education Commissioner nominee, Sidney P. Marland, a "performance contractor." "Teachers and labor forces everywhere must . . . resist attacks on education."

986. "AFT/NEA Merger? Teacher Opinion Poll." *Instructor*, 79 (March, 1970), 43.

   A majority of a random sample of 100 subscribers believes that the AFT would benefit most from a merger.

987. "AFT, NEA Open Talks on Merger." *American Teacher*, 58 (November, 1973), 1+.

   On headquarters discussions in Washington and a local merger in Dade County, Florida.

988. "AFT, NEA Units Merge in Florida." *American Teacher*, 58 (April, 1974), 3.

   Reports the formation of the United Teachers of Florida.

989. "AFT President Shanker Sets Union Priorities." *Library Journal*, 99 (October 15, 1974), 2693.

   A brief report on the new Shanker administration.

990. "The AFT QuEST for Educational Excellence." *American Teacher*, 56 (May, 1972), 1A–15A.

   A supplement devoted to the first national QuEST Consortium, April, 1972, with speeches by Walter Mondale, Wayne Morse, *et al.*

991. "AFT-QuEST '76: The Education Crisis." *American Teacher,* 60 (May, 1976), 13–15.
Fifth Annual AFT-QuEST Consortium, April 23–25, 1976.

992. "AFT-QuEST '77. Education and a New Administration: Expanding the National Commitment." *American Teacher,* 61 (May, 1977), 13–20.
Report on the May 6–8, 1977, QuEST Conference held in Washington, D.C.

993. "AFT Seniors Seek Better Retirement Life." *American Teacher,* 62 (November/December, 1977), 9, 30.
Comments on the first official retirement workshop held at an AFT convention.

994. "AFT Staff to Survey Local's Professional Needs." *American Teacher,* 62 (January, 1978), 4.
A comprehensive review of the AFT's approach to educational and professional issues at the local, state, and national levels is planned.

995. "AFT Steps Up Effort to Stop Ed. Dept. Bill." *American Teacher,* 63 (October, 1978), 1, 6.
AFT has strongly opposed splintering education from its natural allies in the health and welfare communities.

996. "AFT Will Organize Health Professionals." *American Teacher,* 63 (December, 1978/January, 1979), 1, 20.
Report on the first major AFT organizing drive outside the education field.

997. "AFT Wins Berkeley." *American Teacher,* 61 (March, 1977), 1.
The AFT wins a "hotly contested collective bargaining election" over the NEA by a vote of 462 to 333.

998. "AFT Wins University of Connecticut Non-Teaching Staff." *American Teacher,* 61 (December, 1976), 4.
AFT victory over AFSCME for bargaining representation.

999. "AFT's Persistent Press: The Media behind the Message." *American Teacher*, 55 (January, 1971), 8–10.
A survey of local publications.

1000. "Albert Shanker: Power Is Good." *Time*, 106 (September 22, 1975), 17.
Portrait of Shanker with an overview of his positions.

1001. Almy, Timothy A. and Harlan Hahn. "Perceptions of Educational Conflict: The Teacher Strike Controversy in Detroit." *Education and Urban Society*, 3 (August, 1971), 440–452.
Discovers polarization along racial lines and according to whether teacher strikes were perceived as true labor-business conflicts.

1002. "America's Third Century: Meeting Education's Challenges." *American Teacher*, 62 (September, 1977), A1–A28.
Reports on the state of union, 1976–1977, from the officers of the AFT.

1003. " . . . And Two More Colleges Sign On." *American Teacher*, 61 (March, 1977), 4.
Reports on the third straight community college victory in California.

1004. Atkin, J. Myron. "Colleges of Education and the Organized Teaching Profession: A Troubled Relationship." *New York University Education Quarterly*, 7 (Summer, 1976), 8–13. Condensed in *Education Digest*, 42 (November, 1976), 58–61.
Why relations between colleges of education and the organized teaching profession have worsened.

1005. Aussieker, Bill and J. W. Garbarino. "Measuring Faculty Unionism: Quantity and Quality." *Industrial Relations*, 12 (May, 1973), 117–124.
A formularized comparison of the AFT, AAUP, and NEA on college campuses.

1006. Aven, Samuel D. "Professional Associations and Social

Class." *Improving College and University Teaching,* 21 (Summer, 1973), 175+.

Survey finds greatest approval of AFT among male teachers with "blue collar backgrounds."

1007. Badner, George. "Teacher Unity: AFT Style." *Pennsylvania School Journal,* 124 (March, 1976), 112–114+.

History of the NEA–AFT merger and disaffiliation in New York.

1008. "Bakke: Pro and Con (continued): The American Federation of Teachers' *Amicus Curiae* Brief." *Phi Delta Kappan,* 59 (March, 1978), 451–455.

Statement against the quota system. "The decision of the California Supreme Court should be affirmed."

1009. Bard, Bernard. "Albert Shanker: A Portrait in Power." *Phi Delta Kappan,* 56 (March, 1975), 466–472.

Judges Shanker to be an extremely effective, tough, and pragmatic union leader.

1010. Batlin, Carl A. "American Federation of Teachers Endorses Merger Talks with NEA." *Monthly Labor Review,* 96 (October, 1973), 43–44.

Report on the 1973 convention.

1011. Belcher, A. Lee. "The NLRB Ruling: How It Affects Campus Administration." *College and University Business,* 49 (August, 1970), 42–45. See also "The NLRB Asserts Jurisdiction over Private Colleges and Universities." *Journal of the College and University Personnel Association,* 21 (August, 1970), 1–9.

An upsurge of union organizing is predicted.

1012. "Berkeley Staff Holds Firm in Strike Against Cuts." *American Teacher,* 60 (October, 1975), 5.

The first teachers' strike in the school district and Local 1078 receives much public support.

1013. Berry, John N. III. "UFT and/or ALA: Dwindling Community Control of Schools." *Library Journal,* 99 (June 1, 1974), 1503.

147

Argues on the basis of the New York situation that teachers' unions have a place in libraries.

1014. Bhaerman, Robert D. "Accountability: The Great Day of Judgment." *Educational Technology*, 11 (January, 1971), 62–63.
Charges that leading theories of teacher accountability are overly simplistic and educationally unsound.

1015. _____. "INQuEST: An Educational Review." *American Teacher*, 60 (October, 1975), 15, 22; (November, 1975), 21; concluded (December, 1975), 26–27.
Reviews the AFT's role in teacher education.

1016. _____. "Merit Pay? No!" *National Elementary Principal*, 52 (February, 1973), 63–69; reply by Charles D. McKenna, "Merit Pay? Yes!" 69–71.
Argues that merit pay increases are seldom awarded by objective and equitable standards.

1017. _____. "QuEST's New Impact on the Schools." *American Teacher*, 55 (May, 1971), 18–19.
A review of the accomplishments of the QuEST program since 1969.

1018. Birnbaum, Robert. "Unionization and Faculty Compensation." *Educational Record*, 55 (Winter, 1974), 29–33; *Educational Record*, 57 (Spring, 1976), 116–118.
Compares 176 union and non-union colleges and universities and shows the effect collective negotiations have on fringe benefits, salaries, and related matters.

1019. Blum, Albert A. "Research on Teacher Unionism." *Journal of Collective Negotiations in the Public Sector*, 5 (Winter, 1976), 81–96.
Overview of research done since 1962 on public teacher unionization.

1020. Bognanno, Mario F. "Graduate Assistants' Response to Unionization: The Minnesota Experience." *Labor Law Journal*, 27 (January, 1976), 32–37.

An attempt to explain why college and university graduate assistants failed to form a union.

1021. Brody, J. A. "Other Big Teacher Union is Threatening More Strikes This Year, but Defensive Ones." *American School Board Journal*, 163 (October, 1976), 32-34.
Report on the 1976 AFT annual convention focuses on resolutions.

1022. Brown, Ralph S. and Israel Kugler. "Collective Bargaining for the Faculty." *Liberal Education*, 56 (March, 1970), 75-85.
A debate between AFT and AAUP representatives.

1023. Bunzel, John H. "The Faculty Strike at San Francisco State College." *AAUP Bulletin*, 57 (September, 1971), 341-351.
Analysis of the 1969 AFT strike at San Francisco State College.

1024. "California CB Law Signed." *American Teacher*, 60 (October, 1975), 9.
A long-awaited victory for the California Federation of Teachers.

1025. "California: New Frontier for Teacher Bargaining." *American Teacher*, 60 (June, 1976), 12-13.
Discusses the AFT role in winning collective bargaining for California school teachers.

1026. "California Wins First Grievance Arbitration Pact." *American Teacher*, 62 (September, 1977), 7.
The first AFT contract in California to contain binding arbitration is negotiated by San Ysidro Federation of Teachers, Local 3211.

1027. Cheng, Charles W. "Community Participation in Teacher Collective Bargaining: Problems and Prospects." *Harvard Educational Review*, 46 (May, 1976), 153-174.
States that ways exist to include parents and communities in educational decision-making without sacrificing the gains which teachers' unions have won.

1028. "The Children's Lobby." *American Teacher*, 55 (January, 1971), 11+.
Articles by Robert D. Bhaerman, Albert Shanker, et al., presented in connection with the White House Conference on Children.

1029. "Cincinnati Teachers Reject NEA—Bargaining Agent for 15 Years." *American Teacher*, 61 (December, 1976), 3.
Cincinnati Federation of Teachers, Local 1520, ousts the NEA.

1030. Clifford, Peter. "Contracts, Unions, and Collective Bargaining." *Momentum*, 2 (April, 1971), 32–37.
Expresses cautious optimism regarding union bargaining in Catholic schools.

1031. Coe, Alan C. "A Study of the Procedures Used in Collective Bargaining with Faculty Unions in Public Universities." *Journal of the College and University Personnel Association*, 24 (May, 1973), 1–44; 24 (September, 1973), 1–25.
A definitive two-part study from the management side. Includes a bibliography.

1032. Cohodes, Aaron. "Will AASA Turn into a Tiger—or a Pussycat?" *Nation's Schools*, 90 (October, 1972), 26.
School administrators prepare for an AFT–NEA merger.

1033. "Collective Bargaining in 1970—What Teacher Unions Will Demand." *American Teacher*, 54 (January, 1970), 2–5.
A survey of the projected collective bargaining demands of major locals.

1034. "Colleges Spur Bargaining Drive." *American Teacher*, 58 (December, 1973), 1+.
Salaries, tenure quotas, tuition are reported to be among key issues for faculty.

1035. "COMPAS." *American Teacher*, 57 (April, 1973), 1A–7A.
A special supplement on the AFT's over-all plan to meet the educational needs of the schools.

1036. "Contrasting Views on Testing Voiced." *American Teacher*, 62 (March, 1978), 1, 22.

Albert Shanker and NEA President John Ryor exchange opinions at a national conference on achievement testing and basic skills convened by the National Institute of Education.

1037. Coolidge, Jan. "Why Nurses Are Turning to Unions." *American Teacher*, 63 (May, 1979), 5, 10.

Reports on the Federation of Nurses and Health Professionals, affiliated with the AFT.

1038. "Council Hits Mandatory Retirement." *American Teacher*, 62 (October, 1977), 1, 26.

The AFT Executive Council announces that the AFT will fight to remove the discriminatory provisions from the Mandatory Retirement Bill.

1039. "Critical Questions in Education 1974." *American Teacher*, 58 (June, 1974), 11–22.

Speeches and other features by Ralph Nader, Albert Shanker, *et al.*, from the third annual QuEST Consortium.

1040. Damerell, Reginald G. and Maurie Hillson. "If Teachers Merge Into a National Union, They May Have to Work on Their 'Image.' " *American School Board Journal*, 161 (January, 1974), 61–63.

Argues that a giant union may "cripple American education."

1041. _____. "The UFT Tells It Like It Isn't and Makes It Look Like It Is." *Phi Delta Kappan*, 55 (February, 1974), 377–382; see also response by Albert Shanker, pp. 383–387.

Damerell charges that the UFT misleads the public with newspaper advertisements. Shanker says that teachers have a right to explain their case to the public and they deserve to be heard.

1042. Dawson, Paul. "Teacher Militancy and Instructional Media." *AV Communication Review*, 19 (Summer, 1971), 184–197.

Survey reveals that media could become a significant bargaining issue.

1043. "D.C. Strike Ends; Contract Extended." *American Teacher*, 63 (May, 1979), 3.

The twenty-three day strike ends when "no reprisals or adverse actions" are promised by the court.

1044. "Debate! Shanker Confronts NEA Chief on National Radio Show." *American Teacher*, 59 (February, 1975), 17–19+.

The AFT president *vs.* James Harris of the NEA on merger, strikes, quotas.

1045. "Decisive Victory for Overseas Federation." *American Teacher*, 63 (May, 1978), 6.

The Overseas Federation of Teachers maintains its exclusive bargaining rights for 900 teachers in thirty-five Department of Defense schools scattered throughout Europe.

1046. Dewing, Rolland. "The American Federation of Teachers and Desegregation." *Journal of Negro Education*, 42 (Winter, 1973), 79–92.

A survey of AFT policy on desegregation in the 1950s praises the union's leadership.

1047. "DFT Honored at Convention." *American Teacher*, 62 (November/December, 1977), 1, 3.

Mary Ellen Riordan and Theodore Sachs are honored for their roles in a Supreme Court ruling which reaffirmed the constitutional right of public employee unions to negotiate agency shop fees.

1048. "DFT Raps City's Decentralization Plan." *American Teacher*, 62 (March, 1978), 22.

The 1971 decentralization system has increased the bureaucratic problems facing Detroit schools.

1049. Dorros, Sidney. "Teachers as Labor: Teachers as Professionals." *High School Journal*, 54 (April, 1971), 413–421.

The AFT and NEA have become both unions and professional societies.

1050. Downey, Gregg W. "Organized Teachers Soon May Organize Other Public—and Private—Employees." *American School Board Journal*, 164 (October, 1977), 33–36.
Reports on the 1977 AFT convention.

1051. Dupont, Ralph P. and Robert D. Tobin, "Teacher Negotiations into the Seventies." *William and Mary Law Review*, 12 (Summer, 1971), 711–749.
A legal history of negotiations, strikes, and sanctions with recommendations for national legislation and the limited right to strike.

1052. Elam, Stanley M. "Teachers in Politics and the Merger Issue." *Phi Delta Kappan*, 58 (October, 1976), 154.
Report on the August 16, 1976, AFT convention.

1053. "Elect Shanker Vice-President of AFL-CIO." *American Teacher*, 58 (November, 1973), 13+.
Albert Shanker becomes the first teacher member of the AFL-CIO Executive Council.

1054. "Elephant in the House." *Newsweek*, 82 (August 27, 1973), 64.
On Albert Shanker.

1055. Elsila, David. "Unionization: A Labor View." *Educational Leadership*, 29 (December, 1971), 222–224.
The AFT position is explained for an NEA journal.

1056. English, Fenwick. "AFT/NEA Reaction to Staff Differentiation." *Educational Forum*, 36 (January, 1972), 193–198.
Discusses AFT opposition to functional and status categories for teachers.

1057. "Executive Council Makes Eight New Staff Appointments." *American Teacher*, 62 (September, 1977), 8.
Reports on the appointees to the headquarters and the national staff.

1058. Faia, Michael A. "Will Unions Make Us Less Professional?" *College English*, 38 (September, 1976), 1–14.

AFT affiliation does not lower teacher responsibility or professional attitudes.

1059. "The Fight for Female Equality in the Schools." *American Teacher*, 56 (June, 1972), 10–11.
On the AFT's first national conference on "Women in Education," May, 1972.

1060. "First 'Legal' Teachers' Strike Begins." *American Teacher*, 55 (January, 1971), 3+.
Philadelphia Community College, Local 2026, acts in accord with new state legislation.

1061. Fishel, Andrew and Janice Pottker. "Women Teachers and Teacher Power." *Urban Review*, 6 (November–December, 1972), 40–44. Reply by Marjorie Stern, "An Insider's View of the Teachers' Union and Womens' Rights," *Urban Review*, 6 (June–July, 1973), 46–49.
Charges that unions are not responsive to the needs of women teachers. Responds with specific examples of the AFT fight against sex discrimination.

1062. Fishhaut, Erna H. and Donald Pastor. "Should the Public Schools Be Entrusted with Pre-School Education: A Critique of the AFT Proposals." *School Review*, 86 (November, 1977), 38–49. Reply by Laura E. Berk and Minnie P. Berson, with a rejoinder by Fishhaut and Pastor, *School Review*, 87 (November, 1978), 107–124.
Against the AFT plan to "put all early childhood and day care services in the public school."

1063. "Five New England Strikes Come to End." *American Teacher*, 60 (November, 1975), 20.
AFT gains in Massachusetts, Rhode Island, and Connecticut.

1064. "Florida Teacher-Unionists Hold Second Convention Since Merger." *American Teacher*, 60 (May, 1976), 22.
The FEA/United maps plans to represent classified school employees and Florida career service employees in state employment.

1065. Florin, Terence D. "Unionism, An Experiential Report." *New Directions for Community Colleges*, 3 (Autumn, 1975), 29–34.
Discusses conflict between union tactics and the traditional character of the academic community.

1066. Flygare, Thomas J. "Supreme Court Upholds Board's Right to Fire Striking Teachers." *Phi Delta Kappan*, 58 (October, 1976), 206–207.
The Hortonville, Wisconsin, firings are upheld.

1067. "Forging New Alliances for Quality Education; QuEST Conference 78." *American Teacher*, 62 (May, 1978), 17–19, 30.
Reviews the seventh QuEST conference.

1068. "A \$40-Billion Vision of Education for Pre-Schoolers." *U.S. News and World Report*, 80 (June 14, 1976), 42.
Comments on the AFT/AFL-CIO plan for the improvement of pre-school education.

1069. Fox, M. J. and Jim F. Reed. "The Law and Texas Teacher's Unions." *Journal of Collective Negotiations in the Public Sector*, 1 (August, 1972), 269–279.
A general review of AFT progress in the late 1960s, with brief consideration of the situation in Texas.

1070. Fryburg, Estelle L. "Children's Attitudes During the New York City School Strike of 1968." *School and Society*, 98 (November, 1970), 429–433.
A survey reveals that positive attitudes toward school and the teachers survived the strike.

1071. "Gainsville Affiliates!" *American Teacher*, 61 (April, 1977), 8.
The Alachua County Education Association becomes the seventh no-national local to affiliate with the AFT in eighteen months.

1072. "Get Ready for a Lot (a *Lot*) More Pow in Teacher Power." *American School Board Journal*, 161 (October, 1974), 32–37.
Emphasizes similarities between the AFT and the NEA; compares the administrations of Albert Shanker and James Harris.

1073. Gibbons, Russell W. "Union Muscle in Parochial Schools." *Commonweal,* 103 (April 23, 1976), 270.

Report on demands for NLRB elections in Philadelphia, Pittsburgh, Los Angeles, Gary (Indiana), and Kailua (Hawaii).

1074. _____. "Union Muscle in Public Schools." *Commonweal,* 103 (April 23, 1976), 268+.

Comments on the Pittsburgh strike and subsequent agreement of December, 1975–January, 1976.

1075. Glass, Ronald W. "American Federation of Teachers." *Monthly Labor Review,* 93 (October, 1970), 34–36.

A report on the 1970 convention.

1076. "Good News From All Over." *American Teacher,* 61 (February, 1977), 1, 3.

AFT victories in New Jersey and in California.

1077. Greenman, James. "Day Care in the Schools? A Response to the Position of the AFT." *Young Children,* 33 (May, 1978), 4–13.

Supports the AFT Day-Care Plan.

1078. "Grim News Amid the Glitter." *American Teacher,* 60 (December, 1975), 15.

Report on the State Federation Presidents Conference, November, 1975.

1079. Hankin, Joseph N. "What's Past is Prologue." *New Directions for Community Colleges,* 3 (Autumn, 1975), 13–22.

Focuses on collective bargaining in two-year post-secondary institutions.

1080. Harlacher, Frank, Jr. "There's One Gigantic National Teacher Union in Your Future." *American School Board Journal,* 160 (September, 1973), 36–37+.

On the projected AFT–NEA merger and a prediction of its political objectives.

1081. "Hear This: School Boards, Not Teacher Unions, Are in Charge of Schools: the Hortonville Decision." *American School Board Journal,* 163 (August, 1976), 39–41.

The US Supreme Court rules in favor of the Hortonville Board of Education and permits the firing of striking teachers.

1082. Helburn, I. B. "The American Federation of Teachers in Texas: Case Study of a Hostile Environment." *Journal of Collective Negotiations in the Public Sector*, 1 (August, 1972), 203–218.
Reviews union history in Texas since 1902, analyzes the lack of AFT success, and explains why the situation of the locals may improve in the future.

1083. Hellriegel, Don, *et al.* "Collective Negotiations and Teachers: A Behavioral Analysis." *Industrial and Labor Relations Review*, 23 (April, 1970), 380–396.
A study of three Seattle school districts.

1084. "Here's Where the AFT Stands on Current Economic, Educational, and Social Issues." *American Teacher*, 57 (September, 1972), 8–9.
On positions adopted at the 1972 convention.

1085. Hewitt, Malcolm. "Are Teachers Aides Negotiable?" *Journal of Collective Negotiations in the Public Sector*, 1 (November, 1972), 339–345.
A superintendent calls the role of paraprofessionals a "discussable, negotiable issue."

1086. Hill, Velma. "A Profession with Promise." *American Federationist*, 78 (July, 1971), 19–23. Also in *American Teacher*, 56 (October, 1971), 13–15.
Discusses UFT support for the New York City paraprofessional program.

1087. "The Hot-Cold Romance of the Teacher Bosses." *American School Board Journal*, 160 (February, 1973), 8–10+.
On merger problems.

1088. "How Teacher Unions Work." *American Teacher*, 58 (December, 1973), 12–13.
Reports of the November, 1973, national conference of AFT state federations.

1089. "Hucksters in the Schools." *American Teacher*, 55 (September, 1970), 9–11. See also *American Teacher*, 55 (October, 1970), 10–11; *American Teacher*, 55 (November, 1970), 2 and 14–16; *American Teacher*, 56 (January, 1972), 15–17.
On "performance contracting."

1090. "IFT Victories." *American Teacher*, 62 (October, 1977), 5.
The Illinois Federation of Teachers adds four new units to its membership rolls.

1091. "Illinois Teachers Join IFT as Dissatisfaction With IEA Grows." *American Teacher*, 62 (September, 1977), 14.
The IEA loses members; the opposite is true of the IFT.

1092. "Increased Federal Aid is Vital, Teachers Tell 'Outreach' Panel." *American Teacher*, 62 (November/December, 1977), 4.
Teachers in Philadelphia and Baltimore call for full funding for Title I of the Elementary and Secondary Education Act and for increased aid to education.

1093. "The Inflation–Unemployment Squeeze." *American Teacher*, 59 (November, 1974), 15–19.
The union's views on the latest economic recession.

1094. "Is There Really a 'Typical' AFT Member?" *American Teacher*, 54 (April, 1970), 9.
On five recent studies of union membership.

1095. "Judgment Day in the Schools: Trial by Accountability." *American Teacher*, 55 (November, 1970), 11–21.
Articles by Robert D. Bhaerman, Donald A. Collins, Barry R. McGhan, *et al.* on the threat posed by the quest for "efficiency" in the schools.

1096. Kennelly, Jean R. "Collective Bargaining in the Community College." *Educational Record*, 52 (Winter, 1971), 87–92.
Attempts to define basic terms.

1097. Kramer, Edward D. "Grievance Procedures: the Principals'

Role Where There is a Negotiated Contract." *Bulletin of the National Association of Secondary School Principals*, 55 (May, 1971), 159–167.

Advises sensitivity with regard to grievance procedures to avoid union headaches later.

1098. Laarman, Peter. "Conference Tackles Challenges in Organizing Professionals." *American Teacher*, 62 (October, 1977), 6.

Unionists from the AFT, the Retail Clerks, the Government Employees and other affiliates of the Council of AFL-CIO Unions for Professional Employees (CUPE) examine the problems and opportunities they face in organizing professional workers.

1099. _____. "Organizing the Non-Public School Teacher." *American Teacher*, 63 (February, 1979), 7, 20.

Union rights and economic survival are the main issues at stake.

1100. Lambert, Sam M. "NEA Executive Secretary Speaks." *School and Community*, 59 (September, 1972), 12–14+.

Demands an end to labor affiliation as a precondition to merger.

1101. Landsmann, Leanna. " 'Paraprofessionals Are Often the Best PR People Teachers Have'—Shanker." *Instructor*, 83 (November, 1973), 40–42.

In an interview Albert Shanker stresses the common interests of teachers and teachers' aides.

1102. La Noue, George R. and Marvin R. Pilo. "Teacher Unions and Educational Accountability." *Proceedings of the Academy of Political Science*, 30 (December, 1970), 146–158.

Argues for union accommodation on the accountability issue to help maintain public support on salary issues.

1103. Larson, Reed. "Are You Making It Hard for Your Teachers *Not* to Join a Union?" *American School Board Journal*, 159 (March, 1972), 58–61.

Advocates "right-to-work" law protection for non-union teachers.

1104.   Levine, Marvin J. "The Issues in Teacher Strikes." *Journal of General Education*, 22 (April, 1970), 1–18.
Argues that teacher strikes are inevitable without arbitration.

1105.   Lewis, Richard, "Who Will Control the AFT?" *Change*, 6 (May, 1974), 14–17.
Discusses the Shanker–Selden rivalry.

1106.   Lieberman, Myron. "The Future of Collective Negotiations." *Phi Delta Kappan*, 53 (December, 1971), 214–216. Condensed in *Education Digest*, 37 (February, 1972), 1–4.
Predicts a gradual acceptance of collective bargaining throughout the profession and an eventual merger of the AFT and the NEA.

1107.   _____. "NEA-AFT Merger: Breakthrough in New York." *Phi Delta Kappan*, 53 (June, 1972), 622–625.
The state organizations form a congress.

1108.   _____. "Professors, Unite!" *Harper's*, 243 (October, 1971), 61–64+. Condensed in *Current*, 153 (December, 1971), 27–35. Discussion and reply, *Harper's*, 243 (December, 1971), 9–14.
On the AFT as a catalyst in faculty unionization.

1109.   _____. "The Union Merger Movement: Will 3,500,000 Teachers Put It All Together?" *Saturday Review*, 55 (June 24, 1972), 50–56.
Predicts governmental reaction to a united teachers' union.

1110.   _____. "What the Merger Will Mean in Your Negotiations." *School Management*, 18 (February, 1974), 10–12.
Believes merger would "conservatize" the former AFT.

1111.   Lloyd, Ralph. "From Teacher Unity to 'Solidarity Forever': The New York Story." *American Teacher*, 58 (April, 1974), 7.
The old union vs. association arguments are reported to be blurred by common issues.

1112.   "Lobbying and Learning Highlight Para Meeting." *American Teacher*, 62 (May, 1978), 22–23.

Report on the AFT's National Conference on Paraprofessionals held in Washington, D.C., April 27-28, 1978.

1113. Loewenthal, Alfred and Robert Nielsen. "Unions in Aca-
demia: A Bargaining Frontier." *American Federationist*,
84 (April, 1977), 18-23.
Demands and attitudes of collective bargaining on campus.

1114. "Los Angeles Teachers Move toward Merger." *American
Teacher*, 54 (February, 1970), 3+; "AFT Council Calls L.A.
Merger 'Promising Experiment' in Unity," 54 (January, 1970), 7.
On cautious AFT approval of the projected United
Teachers-Los Angeles.

1115. Lubetsky, Kenneth P. "Will the NEA and the AFT Ever
Merge?" *Educational Forum*, 41 (March, 1977), 309-316.
Examines the history of the two organizations, and the
factors which have prevented their merger.

1116. Luria, Jack. "Undermining Bronx High School of Science."
Jewish Frontier, 38 (February, 1971), 9-14.
Why the special school "Bronx Science" was a target for
strike-breaking during the 1968 UFT strike.

1117. McGhan, Barry R. and Charles E. Litz. "The Anatomy of a
Merger." *Phi Delta Kappan*, 51 (June, 1970), 535-539.
Reviews events leading to the merger of the Flint,
Michigan, AFT and NEA.

1118. "McGovern Wins AFT Endorsement." *American Teacher*,
57 (September, 1972), 3+; (October, 1972), 11-12.
The first endorsement of a presidential candidate by the
AFT.

1119. Magarrell, Jack. "Increasing Use of Part-timers Condemned
by Teachers' Union." *Chronicle of Higher Education*, 15
(September 6, 1977), 4.
The position of full-time faculty members is being
undermined and adjunct professors themselves are being
exploited.

1120. "A Major Step Toward Teacher Unity." *American Teacher*, 57 (January, 1973), 1+.
On AFT and NEA cooperation in a National Coalition for Teacher Unity organized to prepare for merger.

1121. Martin, David L. and Philip G. Jones. "How One Small-Town School Board Stood Up To One Big Statewide Teacher Union." *American School Board Journal*, 161 (June, 1974), 16–21.
Hortonville School Board *vs.* the Wisconsin Education Association Council strike.

1122. Mathews, John. "The States Eye NEA–AFT Merger." *Compact*, 8 (January, 1974), 33–35.
Discusses merger in light of possible statewide funding of schools.

1123. "Meany Talks to Teachers." *American Teacher*, 63 (September, 1978), 5, 8.
AFL-CIO President George Meany praises the teachers at the 1978 AFT convention for their participation in the labor movement, and for their militancy at the bargaining table.

1124. Megel, Carl J. and Robert D. Bhaerman. "Teachers Voice Their Opposition." *Compact*, 5 (February, 1971), 31–34.
Discusses the disadvantages of educational vouchers and performance contracting.

1125. "Merger of NEA and AFT Locals." *School and Society*, 98 (January, 1970), 15–16.
On the merger of locals in Flint, Michigan, 1969.

1126. "Militancy Wanes as Teachers Try to Hold on to Jobs." *U.S. News and World Report*, 79 (September 1, 1975), 53–54.
Effect of the job crunch on teacher militancy.

1127. Miller, Charles. "What Is Negotiable?" *Changing Education*, 5 (Fall, 1973), 25–27.
"The demarcation between working conditions and policy is becoming less and less clear."

1128. Miller, Gail. "Beyond Quotas: Toward Reform." *American Teacher*, 60 (February, 1976), 17.
The AFT Human Rights Committee Conference of January 9, 1976, and AFT desegregation efforts.

1129. _____. "Catholic Schools Become New Arena For Union Pioneers." *American Teacher*, 60 (June, 1976), 13, 28.
The union drive in Los Angeles.

1130. _____. "Close-Up: Baltimore." *American Teacher*, 63 (October, 1978), 8-9. See also "Union Scores Victory in Baltimore," *American Teacher*, 63 (December, 1978/January, 1979), 1, 3.
Teachers in Baltimore had been without a bargaining agent since 1976. In 1978 they had the opportunity to elect an organization to represent them.

1131. Mitzman, Barry. "Union Power for Teaching Assistants." *Change*, 7 (June, 1975), 17-19.
History of the growth of teaching assistants associations, specifically at the University of Wisconsin and at the University of Michigan.

1132. "Monroe County, Florida, Teachers Opt for AFT." *American Teacher*, 61 (March, 1977), 4.
The first election is conducted in a combined AFT-NEA local union before national mergers have been concluded.

1133. Moore, William J. "An Analysis of Teacher Union Growth." *Industrial Relations*, 17 (May, 1978), 204-215.
Analyzes the factors influencing teacher union membership.

1134. Moore, William J. and Ray Marshall. "Growth of Teachers' Organizations: A Conceptual Framework." *Journal of Collective Negotiations in the Public Sector*, 2 (August, 1973), 271-297.
Correlates union growth with economic, social, and political factors, and identifies four causes of rapid AFT expansion.

1135. Morrison, Donald E. "Con Con and AFT Merger." *School and Community*, 59 (September, 1972), 23+.
An NEA president urges cooperation with the AFT and the AFL-CIO.

1136. Murphy, Michael J. and Neil Ellman. "The Building Principal and the Union: A Study in Mutual Accommodation." *IAR Research Bulletin*, 14 (June, 1974), 3–5.
On cooperation between principals and AFT locals.

1137. Nagi, Mostafa H. "Social Psychological Correlates of Membership in Teachers' Organizations." *Teachers College Record*, 74 (February, 1973), 369–378.
Concludes that the AFT provides "group security."

1138. "NEA–AFSCME Sign Organizing Pact: AFT to Question." *American Teacher*, 61 (December, 1976), 5.
Colorado and Ohio agreements concern jurisdictional power in organizing teachers and other school personnel.

1139. "NEA Breaks Off Unity Talks." *American Teacher*, 58 (March, 1974), 3–4.
A report plus a press statement by David Selden. State and local mergers are not ruled out.

1140. "NEA Favors Merger Talks." *Monthly Labor Review*, 96 (September, 1973), 89.
A report on the reversal of NEA policy; also compares the strike record of the AFT and NEA.

1141. Nelson, Richard R. "American Federation of Teachers 56th Annual Convention." *Monthly Labor Review*, 95 (October, 1972), 55–56.
A report on the 1972 convention.

1142. "New Orleans Merger Aims at CB Rights." *American Teacher*, 56 (June, 1972), 5+.
On plans for the merger of Local 527 with the Orleans Education Association.

1143. "New York Teacher Marriage Headed For Split." *American Teacher*, 60 (December, 1975), 3–4.
Early report on the disaffiliation movement.

1144. "New York Teachers' Action Ends Hope for Early NEA/AFT Unity." *Phi Delta Kappan*, 57 (Fall, 1976), 424.
The NYSUT Board of Directors votes to disaffiliate with the NEA.

1145. "New York Teachers Favor Cutting Ties With NEA." *American Teacher*, 60 (February, 1976), 3, 16.
Unity between the UFT and the NEA begins to erode.

1146. "New York Teachers Shunning NEA." *American Teacher*, 60 (June, 1976), 4.
Ninety-five percent of the teachers have stayed with the UFT since the March, 1976, severing of the UFT–NEA affiliation.

1147. Newell, R. C. "Protecting Handicapped Teachers." *American Teacher*, 62 (November/December, 1977), 22, 31.
Reports on the new federal regulations dealing with "nondiscrimination on the basis of handicap" and the impact they will have on the teaching profession.

1148. _____. "School Violence: Learning in the Grip of Fear." *American Teacher*, 62 (March, 1978), 6, 7, 24.
Assesses the impact of violence and crime on teaching and learning.

1149. Nigro, Peter D. "What Does a Unionized Faculty Mean?" *College Management*, 5 (January, 1970), 40–41.
Emphasizes non-salary demands by faculty unions.

1150. "140 Teachers Face Christmas in Jail." *American Teacher*, 56 (December, 1971), 6. See also "Newark Teachers Fill County Jail," *American Teacher*, 56 (January, 1972), 3–5; James Lerman, "Thoughts on Prison from Jailed Teacher," *American Teacher*, 56 (February, 1972), 23; "Newark Teach-

ers: Graves, Four Others Released after Three Months of Prison," *American Teacher,* 56 (March, 1972), 4.
Newark teachers serve contempt of court sentences.

1151. "Opinion Poll: In Bargaining Talks, NEA, AFT Sound the Same." *Nation's Schools,* 87 (June, 1971), 35.
An indication that the traditional administration preference for NEA has little effect on real bargaining issues.

1152. "Organizing Teachers in the South." *American Teacher,* 55 (October, 1970), 15–16.
On the establishment and growth of integrated schools.

1153. Osborne, Woodley B., Albert Shanker and John Ryor. "Three Union Leaders Talk About the Academic Future." *Change,* 9 (March, 1977), 30–35.
Unionization of college and university faculty is one of the few areas of growth in higher education.

1154. "Paraprofessionals Choose the AFT." *American Teacher,* 61 (March, 1977), 5.
AFSCME loses to the Michigan Federation of Teachers in Highland Park, Michigan.

1155. "Paraprofessionals: Fastest Growing Force in U.S. Schools." *American Teacher,* 54 (February, 1970), 4–5. See also Bayard Rustin, "Paraprofessional Victory Creates National Impact." *American Teacher,* 55 (November, 1970), 23.
On AFT support for paraprofessionals, provided there are contractual safeguards both for them and for teachers.

1156. "PEF's Right to Represent Unit Upheld." *American Teacher,* 63 (May, 1979), 1, 18.
A unanimous New York State Court of Appeals decision allows the Public Employees Federation, affiliated jointly with the AFT and the Service Employees International Union, AFL-CIO, to represent 46,000 professional, technical, and scientific employees.

1157. "Police-State Tactics Hit N.J. Teachers." *American Teacher,* 54 (February 16, 1970), 1–4. See also "Strike Ends, Contract

Signed," *American Teacher*, 54 (March, 1970), 3–6; David Selden, "Selden Starts 60-Day Prison Term: A Letter from Jail," *American Teacher*, 54 (April, 1970), 1+; David Selden, "A Challenge to the Middle Class: Some Thoughts on Leaving Jail," *American Teacher*, 54 (May, 1970), 2–5, on the jailing of David Selden and others for contempt of court.
Coverage of the Newark strike.

1158.   Polishook, Sheila Stern. "Collective Bargaining and the City University of New York." *Journal of Higher Education*, 41 (May, 1970), 377–386.
Believes that the faculty are learning "to think of themselves as workers."

1159.   "Portland Teachers Bounce NEA: Vote 2–1 to Switch to Federation." *American Teacher*, 56 (October, 1971), 3. See also "Portland Win Reverberates through the West," *American Teacher*, 56 (November, 1971), 12+.
On the AFT victory in Portland, Oregon.

1160.   "Preserving the AFT's History." *American Teacher*, 57 (December, 1972), 20.
On the AFT archival collections at the Walter P. Reuther Library of Labor and Urban Affairs, Wayne State University, Detroit.

1161.   "President Shanker Meets the Press." *American Teacher*, 57 (September, 1974), 20–21.
Excerpts of an NBC television broadcast of September 1, 1974.

1162.   "Professional Unions Elect AFT's Shanker as New President." *American Teacher*, 60 (November, 1975), 12.
The Council of AFL-CIO Unions for Professional Employees elects Shanker.

1163.   "Professionals Get Department in Federation." *American Teacher*, 62 (January, 1978), 1, 7.
Albert Shanker is elected president of the newly formed AFL-CIO's Department of Professional Employees.

1164. "Public Education and Teacher Unions." *Education Digest,* 39 (January, 1974), 48–50.
A National Association of Manufacturers' report calls union membership "unprofessional."

1165. "Public Schools Win Tax Credit Fight." *American Teacher,* 63 (October, 1978), 1, 6.
Albert Shanker hails an "important victory for good public policy and the survival of public education."

1166. "Questions and Answers about More Effective Schools." *American Teacher,* 54 (January, 1970), 16–17. See also Simon Beagle, "MES, a Total School Plan that Works," *American Teacher,* 54 (May, 1970), 11–13; *American Teacher,* 55 (September, 1970), 14.
The AFT sponsored program expands to fifty cities.

1167. Raskin, A. H. "Shanker's Great Leap." *New York Times Magazine,* (September 9, 1973), 64–65+.
Portrait of Albert Shanker as a masterful but increasingly "establishment" union leader.

1168. "Reawakening the Promise of America." *American Teacher,* 61 (September, 1976), C1–C44.
A report on the state of the union (1975–1976) by AFT officers.

1169. Rotigel, David. "Teacher Power, Teacher Unity, and Teacher Professionalism." *Education,* 92 (February, 1972), 76–80.
Advocates an AFT–NEA merger.

1170. Ruby, Michael, et al. "New York's Near D Day." *Newsweek,* 86 (October 27, 1975), 16–19.
The UFT is pressed to save New York City from default.

1171. "St. Louis Teachers Vote for AFT." *American Teacher,* 58 (March, 1974), 5.
Another major city in the union fold.

1172. Sawicki, Robert L. "The Unionization of Professors at the

University of Delaware." *Liberal Education*, 60 (December, 1974), 449–460.
Analyzes an AAUP victory over an AFT campus chapter.

1173. "Schools in Crisis: America's Agenda." *American Teacher*, 63 (September, 1978), A1–A36.
A report on the state of the union, 1977–1978, from the officers of the AFT.

1174. Selden, David. "The American Federation of Teachers Views the Teacher's Changing Role." *Educational Technology*, 10 (February, 1970), 77–80.
Believes teacher militancy is needed to create changes to suit the schools of the future.

1175. ———. "The Myth and the Hope of Teacher Power." In *Association for Supervision and Curriculum Development Yearbook 1974*, pp. 149–154. Washington, D.C.: Association for Supervision and Curriculum, 1974.
Looks toward constructive use of teacher power as basic teacher rights are established.

1176. ———. "Productivity Yes; Accountability No." *Nation's Schools*, 89 (May, 1972), 50–51.
"Teachers do not mind being held accountable for things over which they have some control."

1177. ———. "State of the Union, 1970." *American Teacher*, 55 (September, 1970), 12–13.
Excerpts from a presidential address on militancy, paraprofessionals, organizing in the South.

1178. ———. "Vouchers: Solution or Sop?" *Teachers College Record*, 72 (February, 1971), 365–371.
Charges that voucher plans would polarize American society on racial and religious lines without advancing educational quality for any group.

1179. ———. "Vouchers Unvouchsafed." *Educational Forum*, 37 (November, 1972), 7–12.
Argues that a voucher system would invite teacher

exploitation and other abuses while not guaranteeing better funding for schools.

1180.   Selden, David and Robert D. Bhaerman. "Instructional Technology and the Teaching Profession." *Teachers College Record*, 71 (February, 1970), 391–406.
Indicates that innovation is necessary, but that teachers should be more involved in decisions concerning new technology.

1181.   "Selden, AFT Council Majority in Conflict on Policy Issues." *American Teacher*, 58 (January, 1974), 4–5. See also "Council Restores Democratic Procedures After Selden Refuses to Follow AFT Policy," *American Teacher*, 58 (February, 1974), 2–5.
David Selden is asked to resign over a dispute on union merger policy. Selden defends his actions in an editorial.

1182.   "Settlements Dominate Strike Scene." *American Teacher*, 63 (October, 1978), 5, 7.
The Cleveland, Ohio, and Levittown, New York, strikes continue, but the AFT's bargaining expertise pays off as other strikes are settled with improved pacts.

1183.   Shanker, Albert. "An AFT Program for Lifelong Education." *American Teacher*, 59 (October, 1974), 16–17.
An address to the National Press Club, September 24, 1974.

1184.   _____. "Ford *vs.* New York City: A Reckless Gamble." *American Teacher*, 60 (November, 1975), 6.
Criticizes the president's stand on the New York financial crisis.

1185.   _____. "Massive Action Needed to Stop Tuition Tax Credit Bill." *American Teacher*, 62 (April, 1978), 3.
An open letter to AFT members.

1186.   _____. "Teacher Unity in Perspective." *American Teacher*, 61 (September, 1976), A2.
A review of the past sixty years of the AFT.

1187. _____. "Where We Stand: An Integrated . . . or Totalitarian . . . Society?" *New York Times*, October 9, 1977, Section 4, p. 7.

An open letter to Senator Javits asking for an end to the strict distribution of teachers throughout the schools on a racial basis.

1188. _____. "Where We Stand: Bilingual Education Must Be Expanded." *New York Times*, May 28, 1978, Section 4, p. 7.

The major effort of a bilingual program should be to help children learn to speak English after which instruction should be conducted in English. Using the bilingual program to establish permanent national and ethnic enclaves in the schools does the children an injustice.

1189. _____. "Where We Stand: Day Care—We Lag Far Behind Europe." *New York Times*, June 10, 1979, Section 4, p. E7.

The United States lags far behind European countries in addressing the problem of how to care for the very young children of working parents.

1190. _____. "Where We Stand: For Teachers and Unions, A New High in Political Action and a New Need for Vigilance." *New York Times*, October 22, 1972, Section 4, p. 9.

Discusses the importance of the 1972 election for the labor movement.

1191. _____. "Where We Stand: HEW Threatens to Make Children Pay." *New York Times*, September 11, 1977, Section 4, p. 9.

The hiring of teachers based upon competency as determined by written tests should be continued.

1192. _____. "Where We Stand: High Court Limits Public Employee Rights." *New York Times*, June 27, 1976, Section 4, p. 9.

Second-class citizenship for public workers.

1193. _____. "Where We Stand: How Safe Are Public Employee Pensions?" *New York Times*, February 22, 1976, Section 4, p. 7.

Calls for congressional action to provide federal protection for public employee pension funds.

1194. _____. "Where We Stand: Is Tax Cut Fever Sweeping the Country?" *New York Times*, June 18, 1978, Section 4, p. 9.

Although a majority of Americans feel that state and property taxes are too high, even larger majorities feel that the state governments are spending too little on social services. The mandated California cuts in state taxes produce increases in federal taxes. The message from the voters is, therefore, unclear.

1195. _____. "Where We Stand: Leaving Students Back Is Not Enough." *New York Times*, November 20, 1977, Section 4, p. 7.

The failing of students who do not reach a certain level of achievement is labeled an educational "quick fix" which did not eliminate functional illiteracy when it was tried before and will not work today. Individualized instruction in classes of twenty or fewer students is what is needed.

1196. _____. "Where We Stand: Most Can Learn Under Right Conditions." *New York Times*, April 17, 1977, Section 4, p. 11.

A book review of *Human Characteristics and School Learning* (New York: McGraw Hill, 1976) by Professor Benjamin S. Bloom. Bloom maintains schools can and do make a difference and that " . . . most students can achieve a 'A' level of mastery if taught systematically and appropriately, with the emphasis on individualized instruction."

1197. _____. "Where We Stand: 1978 Agenda for Action in Washington." *New York Times*, January 1, 1978, Section 4, p. 5.

A call for more jobs, welfare reform, national health program, low interest loans to cities, increased federal aid to education, and labor law reform.

1198. _____. "Where We Stand: Now, More Than Ever, Teachers Need Unity—And Labor Support." *New York Times*, May 12, 1974, Section 4, p. 11.

Blatant attempts to crush two small-district locals are reported, new warnings of the need for solidarity.

1199. _____. "Where We Stand: Proposition 13: What Does It Mean?" *American Teacher*, 63 (September, 1978), 4.
Assesses the impact of Proposition 13.

1200. _____. "Where We Stand: Speaking Out Against a Separate Department of Education." *American Teacher*, 63 (April, 1979), 8-9.
"American schools have problems, of course, especially in educating the urban poor. But they won't be solved by a new bureaucracy in Washington."

1201. _____. "Where We Stand: Supreme Court Upholds Residency Law But City Would Be Unwise to Adopt It." *New York Times*, April 25, 1976, Section 4, p. 5.
Some of the consequences of cities enacting residency requirements for their employees.

1202. _____. "Where We Stand: Teacher Unionism: A Quiet Revolution Now Enters a Wider Arena." *New York Times*, October 28, 1973, Section 4, p. 9.
Argues that AFT programs should be judged in the wider context of efforts toward a more just and decent society.

1203. _____. "Where We Stand: Teacher Unity: Present Hopes Dashed, but the Need Persists." *New York Times*, March 3, 1974, Section 4, p. 7.
"The merger question will remain alive so long as teachers and schools face the problems they do."

1204. _____. "Where We Stand: Teachers' Rights: Good Progress, but the Fight is Far from Won." *New York Times*, December 23, 1973, Section 4, p. 7.
Despite hard-won union victories, serious efforts still are made to restrict teacher civil rights.

1205. _____. "Where We Stand: Teachers Save City, but Rescue Is Temporary." *New York Times*, October 19, 1975, Section 4, p. 7.
The UFT rescues New York City from default.

1206. _____. "Where We Stand: The Public's View of the Public Schools." *New York Times*, September 16, 1973, Section 4, p. 9.
  The public does not agree with the assertion of the critics that the public schools are failures.

1207. _____. "Where We Stand: The School Board as 'Sovereign': An Outmoded Idea." *New York Times*, April 13, 1975, Section 4, p. 9.
  Comments on a survey by the National School Boards Association indicating loss of confidence in local boards.

1208. _____. "Where We Stand: The Teachers Are Learning Labor's Lessons." *New York Times*, February 2, 1975, Section 4, p. 7.
  Urges support for the AFL-CIO's "Action Plan" to fight the recession.

1209. _____. "Where We Stand: Why Does NEA Resist Full Disclosure?" *American Teacher*, 63 (February, 1979), 8.
  The NEA should comply with the 1959 Labor-Management Reporting and Disclosure Act.

1210. _____. "Why Teachers Are Angry." *American School Board Journal*, 162 (January, 1975), 23–26. See also Bruce A. Richardson, "Listen, Mr. Shanker, It's not Quite as Simple as You Make It Sound," *American School Board Journal*, 162 (May, 1975), 46, 49.
  Condemns the oppressive paternalism of school boards, argues for just remuneration and professional dignity.

1211. _____. "Why Teachers Need the Right to Strike." *Monthly Labor Review*, 96 (September, 1973), 48–51.
  Argues that the freedom of employees in the private sector should be extended to public employees.

1212. "Shanker and Herndon Debate On School Discipline, Testing." *American Teacher*, 62 (September, 1977), 4.
  The third in an annual series of debates between the leaders of the AFT and the NEA.

1213. "Shanker Appears on Televised Debate." *American Teacher*, 62 (May, 1978), 9.
Shanker voices his opposition to the tuition tax credit proposal.

1214. "Shanker Calls for United Action." *American Teacher*, 61 (April, 1977), 7.
Urges education organizations on both sides of the bargaining table to work together towards a national agreement on the scope of collective bargaining in schools.

1215. "Shanker Challenges City Bosses on Public-Employee Bargaining." *American Teacher*, 60 (February, 1976), 20, 23.
Shanker's speech at the National League of Cities' Labor–Management Service Conference, January 12–13, 1976.

1216. "Shanker, Herndon Air Issues and Differences." *American Teacher*, 61 (September, 1976), A7.
A radio debate between Albert Shanker and NEA Executive Secretary Terry Herndon.

1217. "Shanker in Debate on Testing." *American Teacher*, 62 (October, 1977), 8, 22.
Shanker, Willard Wirtz and Dr. Frank E. Armbruster discuss testing and the decline in test scores.

1218. "Shanker Raps Proposed Education Department." *American Teacher*, 62 (February, 1978), 4.
President Carter's announcement of support for a separate Department of Education draws sharp criticism from Albert Shanker.

1219. "Shanker Testifies on Education Dept." *American Teacher*, 63 (May, 1979), 3.
Anti-Education Department testimony before the House Government Operations Committee, Subcommittee on Legislation and National Security.

1220. Sherman, Robert R., et al. "Loyalty in Florida, 1969." *Changing Education*, 4 (Spring, 1970), 18–22.

On the efforts of AFT members at the University of Florida to abolish loyalty oaths.

1221. "Should Your Teacher Strike?" *American Teacher,* 54 (May, 1970), 1A–8A.
A supplement devoted to three lessons for schools on the rights of public employees.

1222. Sibelman, Larry. "Merger in Los Angeles." *American Teacher,* 56 (October, 1971), 24.
A discussion of the effectiveness of the combined Los Angeles teachers union by the union leader who engineered the merger.

1223. Sill, Geoffrey. "Democracy in the AFT?" *Nation,* 223 (July 3, 1976), 6.
Shanker attempts to consolidate power at the August, 1976, AFT convention by dissolving Local 189.

1224. Simon, Larry G. "The School Finance Decisions: Collective Bargaining and Future Finance Systems." *Yale Law Journal,* 82 (January, 1973), 409–460.
Discusses the impact on teachers' unions of state government school financing of public schools.

1225. Simons, William H. "Union Proposals for Washington Schools." *Integrated Education,* 8 (September–October, 1970), 50–52.
A statement prepared for the Senate Committee on the District of Columbia by the president of the Washington Teachers Union.

1226. "Staff Changes Approved by Council." *American Teacher,* 63 (February, 1979), 22.
New appointments to AFT headquarters and field staff.

1227. "Starting the 12-Month Countdown." *American Teacher,* 56 (November, 1971), 15–17.
"AFT launches a political-action drive to unfreeze Congress, the White House, and state legislatures in 1972."

1228. Stern, Marjorie. "Teacher Unions and Women's Rights." *American Teacher*, 55 (June, 1971), 6.
A discussion of two resolutions passed at the 1970 AFT convention.

1229. "Summary of State Collective Bargaining Statutes Affecting Teachers." *Compact*, 5 (February, 1971), 17-24.
Surveys the legal climate of AFT locals by states but without specific mention of the union.

1230. "SUNY Election Landmark Victory for AFT." *American Teacher*, 63 (February, 1979), 1, 18.
The NEA is defeated by 2,000 votes by the United University Professions, AFT, Local 2190. The UUP retains the bargaining rights for 16,000 professional and academic employees of the State University of New York.

1231. Suttles, Al. "Victory in Connecticut." *American Teacher*, 60 (April, 1976), 23.
After defeats in 1968 and 1972 the Stamford Federation of Teachers wins bargaining rights in 1976.

1232. "Talking Union." *Newsweek*, 77 (June 14, 1971), 76-77.
A report on college faculty organization.

1233. "Task Force Reviews Federal Regs." *American Teacher*, 63 (February, 1979), 5.
A newly-formed AFT special committee, the AFT Educational Issues Task Force on the 1978 Elementary and Secondary Education Amendments, convened for the first time on January 5, 1979, at the AFT national office to analyze proposed federal regulations.

1234. "Teachers and Unions." *Newsweek*, 80 (September 4, 1972), 54-55.
On the possibility of an AFT-NEA merger.

1235. "Teachers Blast Nixon's Freeze." *American Teacher*, 56 (September, 1971), 3-4.
An AFT-sponsored emergency conference in Washington protests the wage freeze.

1236. "Teachers Face Fines, Imprisonment." *American Teacher*, 63 (April, 1979), 1, 5.
A report on the AFT, Local 6, Washington Teachers Union.

1237. "Teachers' Merger Talks Fail." *Monthly Labor Review*, 97 (May, 1974), 81.
A short report on the impasse between the AFT and the NEA.

1238. "Teachers Open Drive to Sell Unionism." *U.S. News and World Report*, 68 (May 18, 1970), 88.
Report concerns the AFT's instructional materials on public employee unions.

1239. "Teachers Pick AFT in Alaska." *American Teacher*, 63 (February, 1979), 19.
Valdez Local 3479 wins in a thirty-five to thirty-two vote.

1240. "Teachers Strike in Puerto Rico." *American Teacher*, 58 (March, 1974), 1+.
On the first AFT strike in the island commonwealth.

1241. "Teachers Tackle Top Education Issues." *American Teacher*, 62 (May, 1978), 18, 19, 30.
Reports on the 1978 QuEST Conference.

1242. "Teachers' Unions Step Toward Unity." *Business Week*, January 10, 1970, pp. 36–38.
Report focuses on preparations for the Los Angeles AFT–NEA merger.

1243. "A 'Teachers' War' That's Costing Millions." *U.S. News and World Report*, 80 (April 5, 1976), 90–91.
Comments that the NEA and the AFT are more concerned about doing each other in than uniting and solving problems and saving millions.

1244. "Texas Federation Makes Big Gains in Legislative 'Lobby Day' Drives." *American Teacher*, 62 (September, 1977), 17.
Reports on problems faced by Texas teachers in their lobbying efforts.

1245. "Top IEA District Joins Federation Ranks." *American Teacher,* 62 (November/December, 1977), 5.
Six hundred high school teachers in Cook County's District 211 vote by a 77 percent margin to affiliate with the IFT/AFT.

1246. "Toward a More Effective High School." *American Teacher,* 54 (May, 1974), 19–24.
On the AFT's Comprehensive Program for American Schools, an intensive investigation into reforms and new teaching methods.

1247. "Union Man." *Time,* 99 (May 29, 1972), 47+.
A portrait of Albert Shanker.

1248. "Unionization of Faculty Expected to Pick Up Speed Because of Tight Money and Ph.D.'s." *College Management,* 6 (September, 1971), 38.
Reports on "unprecedented" campus unionization.

1249. "Unionizing College Faculties." *Saturday Review,* 54 (June 19, 1971), 52.
Reports on AFT progress on American campuses.

1250. "Unions Woo the College Faculties." *Business Week,* May 1, 1971, pp. 69–74.
A review of the aims of the AFT and its rivals on American campuses.

1251. "Victory in St. Louis as Teachers End Strike." *American Teacher,* 63 (April, 1979), 1, 17.
A fifty-six day strike ends with impressive gains for teachers and paraprofessionals.

1252. Ward, Douglas. "Union Security in Teacher Contracts." *Labor Law Journal,* 22 (March, 1971), 157–172.
A significant lexicon of terms regarding contract security arrangements.

1253. Weiner, Lois. "Cracks in Shanker's Empire." *New Politics,* 11 (Fall, 1976), 51–57.

Shanker's policies are attacked by a radical member of Local 1423, Hayward, California.

1254. _____. "Unions on the Brink: Deathwish Among the Teachers." *Nation*, 225 (September 24, 1977), 276–277.
Assesses the 1977 AFT convention and the future of the AFT.

1255. Weintraub, Andrew R. and Robert J. Thornton. "Why Teachers Strike: The Economic and Legal Determinants." *Journal of Collective Negotiations in the Public Sector*, 5 (No. 3, 1976), 193–206.
Investigates the pattern of strikes among public school teachers in the United States from 1946 to 1973.

1256. Wenrich, William J. "Collective Bargaining: A Special Case for Vocational Education." *American Vocational Journal*, 49 (October, 1974), 31–33.
Points out certain issues (fixed salary schedules, restricted workloads) which, if subject to negotiation, can wreak havoc with vocational programs.

1257. "What the Teacher Unions Have in Store for You." *American School Board Journal*, 162 (September, 1975), 32–38.
"The NEA and the AFT . . . are determined to dominate public education in the U.S."

1258. "What's Happening in the More Effective Schools?" *American Teacher*, 56 (November, 1971), 19.
On re-evaluation of the successful MES program of the seventies.

1259. "What's This?" *American School Board Journal*, 158 (July, 1970), 5.
A comment on a settlement by Los Angeles teachers foregoing raises for a reduction in class size.

1260. "Why We Went on Strike." *American Teacher*, 60 (October, 1975), 10–11.
Statements from Chicago, New York City, Berkeley (California), Waukegan (Illinois), and Wilmington (Delaware).

1261. Wollett, Donald H. "Trends in the Law of Collective Negotiations in Education." *Popular Government*, 36 (April, 1970), 1-6.

Surveys a decade of legal precedents concerning collective bargaining and teacher strikes; envisions nationwide teacher unionism.

III. DISSERTATIONS AND THESES

1262. Anderson, Olive Orton. "The Chicago Teachers' Federation." M.A. thesis, University of Chicago, 1908.

1263. Bitner, William Lawrence. "An Examination of the Organization of American Federation of Teachers Locals in Selected Suburban Communities." Ed.D. dissertation, New York University, 1964.

1264. Browder, Lesley Hughs, Jr. "Teacher Unionism in America: A Descriptive Analysis of the Structure, Force, and Membership of the American Federation of Teachers." Ed.D. dissertation, Cornell University, 1965.

1265. Caliguri, Joseph. "A Comparison of the Relationships between Two Types of Teachers' Organizations and the Superintendent and School Board." Ph.D. dissertation, University of Chicago, 1963.

1266. Christensen, John Edward. "A History of Teacher Unions." M.A. thesis, Arizona State Teachers College, 1940.

1267. Clancy, Lynn Roger, Jr. "The History of the American Federation of Teachers in Los Angeles, 1919–1969." Ph.D. dissertation, University of California, Los Angeles, 1971.

1268. Clark, Robert L. "The Roles and Positions of the NEA and of the AFT in Collective Negotiations: Opinions of Teachers and School Administrators of Five Selected School Districts in Illinois." Ph.D. dissertation, Southern Illinois University, 1965.

1269. Clarke, James Earl. "The American Federation of Teachers: Origins and History from 1870 to 1952." Ph.D. dissertation, Cornell University, 1966.

1270. Close, William Edward. "An Historical Study of the American Federation of Labor–Congress of Industrial Organizations Involvement in Higher Education with an Emphasis on the Period 1960-1969." Ph.D. dissertation, Catholic University of America, 1972.

1271. Craft, James Arthur. "An Analysis of Collective Negotiations in California Public Education." Ph.D. dissertation, University of California, Berkeley, 1968.

1272. Dewing, Rolland Lloyd. "Teacher Organizations and Desegregation, 1959–1964." Ph.D. dissertation, Ball State University, 1967.

1273. Eaton, William Edward. "The Social and Educational Position of the American Federation of Teachers, 1929–1941." Ph.D. dissertation, Washington University, 1971.

1274. Fordyce, Wellington G. "The Origin and Development of Teachers' Unions in the United States." Ph.D. dissertation, Ohio State University, 1945.

1275. Gilmer, Mary Fant. "History, Activities, and Present Status of the Atlanta Public School Teachers' Association." M.A. thesis, Emory University, 1939.

1276. Goergen, Joseph Henry and John Joseph Keough. "Issues and Outcomes of Teachers' Strikes, 1955–1965." Ph.D. and Ed.D. dissertations, St. John's University, 1967.

1277. Goulding, Joel Arthur. "The History of Unionism in American Higher Education." Ed.D. dissertation, Wayne State University, 1970.

1278. Graybiel, John M. "The American Federation of Teachers, 1916–1928." M.A. thesis, University of California, 1928.

1279. Gsell, Donald Albert. "Teacher Unionism in New Jersey: A History and Current Analysis." Ed.D. dissertation, Rutgers University, 1968.

1280. Hobbs, Edward Henry. "The American Federation of Teachers: A Study in Politics and Administration." M.A. thesis, University of Alabama, 1947.

1281. Keough, John Joseph. See entry #1276.

1282. Kochman, Philip. "The Developing Role of Teacher

Unions." Ed.D. dissertation, Teachers College, Columbia University, 1947.

1283. Lester, Jeanette. "The American Federation of Teachers in Higher Education: A History of Union Organization of Faculty Members in Colleges and Universities, 1916–1966." Ed.D. dissertation, University of Toledo, 1968.

1284. Levitan, Sar A. "A Study of the American Federation of Teachers." M.A. thesis, Columbia University, 1939.

1285. Levitt, Emma. "The Activities of Local Teacher Organizations in Chicago since 1929." M.A. thesis, University of Chicago, 1936.

1286. Lowman, Fern Elizabeth. "The Rise, Objectives, and Mode of Operation of the American Federation of Teachers." M.A. thesis, State University of Iowa, 1945.

1287. McLaughlin, Samuel J. "The Educational Policies and Activities of the American Federation of Labor during the Present Century." Ph.D. dissertation, New York University, 1936.

1288. Miller, Charles William. "Democracy in Education: A Study of How the American Federation of Teachers Met the Threat of Communist Subversion through the Democratic Process." Ed.D. dissertation, Northwestern University, 1967.

1289. Miller, Oscar Edward. "A Comparative Study, as to Organization and Functions, of the San Antonio Teachers Council with Local Teacher Associations in Cities of the United States, of 100,000 Population or More." M.A. thesis, University of Texas, 1936.

1290. Morris, Francis Neal. "A History of Teacher Unionism in the State of Washington 1920–1945." M.A. thesis, University of Washington, 1968.

1291. Muffoletto, Anna May. "Detroit Public-School Teachers' Unions: Organization, Operation, and Activities." M.A. thesis, University of Detroit, 1958.

1292. Nottenburg, Robert A. "The Relationship of Organized Labor to Public School Legislation in Illinois, 1880–1948." Ph.D. dissertation, University of Chicago, 1950.

1293. Oakes, Russell Curtis. "Public and Professional Reactions to Teachers' Strikes, 1918–1954." Ed.D. dissertation, New York University, 1958.

1294. Pearse, Robert Francis. "Studies in White Collar Unionism; The Development of a Teachers Union." Ph.D. dissertation, University of Chicago, 1950.

1295. Peterson, Richard Earl. "An Analysis of the Goals of the National Education Association and of the American Federation of Teachers." Ed.D. dissertation, St. John's University, 1967.

1296. Pottishman, Nancy. "Jane Addams and Education." M.A. thesis, Columbia University, 1960.

1297. Reid, Robert Louis. "The Professionalization of Public School Teachers: The Chicago Experience 1895–1920." Ph.D. dissertation, Northwestern University, 1968.

1298. Roat, David Harold. "Professionalization and the Michigan Federation of Teachers, an Analysis of Activities and Structure." Ph.D. dissertation, Michigan State University, 1968.

1299. Salerno, Michael Philip. "A Study of Various Aspects of Teacher Unionism in the United States." Ph.D. dissertation, University of Wyoming, 1967.

1300. Salz, Arthur Eliot. "The Growth of Teacher Unionism in New York City, 1945–1962." Ed.D. dissertation, Columbia University, 1968.

1301. Schiff, Albert. "A Study and Evaluation of Teachers' Strikes in the United States." Ed.D. dissertation, Wayne State University, 1952.

1302. Skibbens, Charles Paul. "The Teachers Union: A Study of Its

Programs, Problems, and Possibilities." M.S. thesis, Loyola University, 1956.

1303. Tomlinson, James L. "Teacher Organization and Labor Affiliation With the Educational Activities of the American Federation of Labor." M.A. thesis, Cornell University, 1944.

1304. Tostberg, Robert Eugene. "Educational Ferment in Chicago, 1883–1904." Ph.D. dissertation, University of Wisconsin, 1960.

1305. Waskiewicz, Leon S. "Organized Labor and Public Education in Michigan from 1880 to 1938." Ph.D. dissertation, University of Michigan, 1939.

1306. Welsh, James W. "A Brief History of the Union Movement among Teachers in the Public Schools of the United States." M.A. thesis, University of Michigan, 1930.

IV. SELECTED AFT DOCUMENTS AND PAMPHLETS

Note: Many of the following are located in the AFT collections of the Walter P. Reuther Library of Labor and Urban Affairs, Wayne State University, Detroit, Michigan, herafter cited as WSU. Others are available from ERIC Document Reproduction Service (EDRS), P.O.B. 190, Arlington, Va. 22210.

BEFORE 1960

1307. American Federation of Teachers. "Accomplishments of the A.F.T." Chicago, Illinois, 1938. WSU AFT Collection, Series I, Box 68.

1308. _____. "British Teachers and the War." Chicago, Illinois, 1942. WSU AFT Collection, Series I, Box 68.

1309. _____. "Constitution of the American Federation of Teachers." Chicago, Illinois, 1933. WSU St. Paul Federation of Teachers Collection, Box 2.

1310. _____. "Fringe Benefits for Teachers: Sick Leave, Health Insurance Longevity Increments." Chicago, Illinois, 1958. WSU AFT Collection, Series I, Box 71.

1311. _____. "Handbook for Building Representatives." Chicago, Illinois, 1959. WSU AFT Collection, Series I, Box 7.

1312. _____. "Information about the A.F.T." Chicago, Illinois, 1938. WSU AFT Collection, Series I, Box 68.

1313. _____. "The Jerome Davis Case: Final Report of an Investigation Conducted by the American Federation of Teachers into the Proposed Dismissal of Professor Jerome Davis from the Stark Chair of Practical Philanthropy at the Yale Divinity School." Chicago, Illinois, 1937. WSU AFT Collection, Series XII, Box 90.

1314. _____. "Manual for Locals." Chicago, Illinois, 1959. WSU AFT Collection, Series V, Box 6.

1315. _____. "Merit Rating: A Dangerous Mirage or Master Plan?" Chicago, Illinois, 1958. WSU AFT Collection, Series V, Box 6.

1316. _____. "Policies of the A.F.T." Chicago, Illinois, 1956. WSU AFT Collection, Series V, Box 5.

1317. _____. "A Program of Action for Classroom Teachers." Chicago, Illinois, 1938. WSU AFT Collection, Series I, Box 68.

1318. _____. "Tales of Ten Cities: Stories of Programs of Action and Actual Accomplishments of Typical Locals of the American Federation of Teachers in Ten Representative Cities of Various Size." Chicago, Illinois, 1942. WSU AFT Collection, Miscellaneous Publications, R–Z.

1319. American Federation of Teachers. National Academic Committee. "The Keeney Case; Big Business, Higher Education, and Organized Labor: Report of an Investigation Made by the National Academic Freedom Committee of the American Federation of Teachers into the Causes of the Recent Dismissal of Professor Philip O. Keeney, Librarian, from Montana State University and the Role Played by Certain Business and Political Interests in the Affairs of the University." Chicago, Illinois, 1939. WSU St. Paul Federation of Teachers Collection, Box 2.

1320. Baker, Frank. "Teachers Should Organize." Chicago, Illinois, 1938. WSU AFT Collection, Series I, Box 68.

1321. California State Federation of Teachers. "Can Teachers' Unions Be Called Out on Strike?" Chicago, Illinois, 1938. WSU AFT Collection, Series I, Box 68.

1322. Davis, Jerome. "Six Reasons for Joining the A.F.T." Chicago, Illinois, 1938. WSU AFT Collection, Series I, Box 68.

1323. Dewey, John. "The Crisis in Education." Chicago, Illinois, 1933. WSU AFT Collection, Series I, Box 68.

1324. Greve, Florence Roehm. "Survey of Salaries Paid in

Representative American Universities and Teacher Training Schools; Survey of Salaries Paid in Junior Colleges in the United States." Chicago, Illinois, 1956. WSU AFT Collection, Series I, Box 58.

1325. Hardy, Ruth Gillette. "The Historical Setting of the A.F.T." Chicago, Illinois, 1938. WSU AFT Collection, Series I, Box 68.

1326. Herrick, Mary. "Discipline: What For and How?" Chicago, Illinois, 1957. WSU Mary Herrick Collection, Series III, Box 3.

1327. _____. "Television: Tool for Education or Substitute." Chicago, Illinois, 1958. WSU Mary Herrick Collection, Series III, Box 3.

1328. Linville, Henry R. "Oaths of Loyalty for Teachers." Chicago, Illinois, 1935. WSU AFT Collection, Series I, Box 69.

1329. McCoy, W. T. "Report of the Better Schools Service." Chicago, Illinois, 1921. WSU AFT Collection, Series I, Box 69.

1330. Megel, Carl J. "Goals of the AFL–CIO American Federation of Teachers and Why." Chicago, Illinois, 1959. WSU AFT Collection, Series I, Box 68.

1331. Reuter, George S., Jr. "Personnel Relations for Teachers." Chicago, Illinois, 1959. WSU AFT Collection, unprocessed material.

1332. Stillman, Charles B. "A Call to Action: Constitution Adopted at the Third Convention." Chicago, Illinois, 1918. WSU AFT Collection, Series I, Box 68.

1333. Stillman, Charles B., et al. "Statement of Principles, March 13, 1978: Democracy in Education—Education for Democracy." Chicago, Illinois, 1918. WSU AFT Collection, Series I, Box 68.

1334. Swope, Ammon, et al. "A Survey of Vocational Education in the United States for the American Federation of Teachers." Chicago, Illinois, 1956. WSU AFT Collection, Series I, Box 18.

1335. TUCNY, Local 5. "The College Teacher and the Trade Union." New York, New York, 1935. WSU AFT Collection, Local 5 Miscellaneous Publications.

1336. Ward, Paul D. "Legislative Handbook: Federal and State Aid, Collective Bargaining, Tenure, Teacher-Rights, Fringe Benefits. A Guide to a Complete Legislative Program." Chicago, Illinois, 1959. WSU AFT Collection, Series V, Box 6.

1960-1969

1337. American Federation of Teachers. "A Brief Historical Review of the American Federation of Teachers' Fight for Integration." Chicago, Illinois, 1964. WSU AFT Collection, Series I, Box 71.

1338. _____. "Building Rep Handbook." Chicago, Illinois, 1966. WSU AFT Collection, Miscellaneous Publications, A–L.

1339. _____. "Collective Bargaining Contracts Negotiated by Locals of the American Federation of Teachers, AFL-CIO." Chicago, Illinois, 1962. WSU Mary Herrick Collection, Series VI, Box 4.

1340. _____. "The North East Regional Conference on Quality Educational Standards in Teaching: Summary Findings (Albany, March 7-8, 1969). QuEST Report Series, #1." Washington, D.C., 1969. Available from ERIC, Document #ED 032 267.

1341. _____. "Selected Opinions Concerning the National Defense Education Act." Chicago, Illinois, 1960. WSU AFT Collection, Miscellaneous Publications, R–Z.

1342. _____. "A Survey of Legislative Action in the State Legislatures Concerning Education." Chicago, Illinois, 1962. WSU AFT Collection, unprocessed material.

1343. _____. "The Teacher and General Education." Chicago, Illinois, 1961. WSU AFT Collection, unprocessed material.

1344. Axtelle, George E. "Teacher Organization and Democracy in School Administration." Chicago, Illinois, 1966. WSU Selma Borchardt Collection, Box 143.

1345. Beagle, Simon. "Evaluating MES: A Survey of Research on the More Effective Schools Plan." Washington, D.C., 1969. Available from ERIC, Document #ED 044 471.

1346. Bhaerman, Robert D. "Education's New Dualisms: A Provocative Essay on Paraprofessionals and Professionalism. QuEST Series 8." Washington, D.C., 1969. Available from ERIC, Document #ED 036 457.

1347. _____. "Needed: A Conceptual Framework for Collective Bargaining in Education. AFT QuEST Paper No. 9." Washington, D.C., 1969. Available from ERIC, Document #ED 038 370.

1348. _____. "Quality Teaching: Some New Thoughts on AFT's Role in Inservice Education. QuEST Papers Series, #3." Washington, D.C., 1969. Available from ERIC, Document #ED 032 270.

1349. _____. "The Role of the AFT in Teacher Education. QuEST Papers Series, #1." Washington, D.C., 1969. Available from ERIC, Document #ED 032 268.

1350. _____. "Several Educators' Cure for the Common Cold, Among Other Things, or, One Unionist's View of Staff Differentiation." Washington, D.C., 1969. Available from ERIC, Document #ED 029 825.

1351. _____. "Which Way for Teacher Certification? QuEST Papers Series, #2." Washington, D.C., 1969. Available from ERIC, Document #ED 032 269.

1352. Bhaerman, Robert D., ed. "AFT QuEST Report on Differentiated Staffing." Washington, D.C., 1969. Available from ERIC, Document #ED 033 914.

1353. Bhaerman, Robert D. and David Selden. "Instructional Technology and the Teaching Profession. QuEST Papers Series, #6." Washington, D.C., 1969. Available from ERIC, Document #ED 032 238.

1354. Burton, Donald B. "The Earning Power of Teachers: A Comparative Analysis of the Economic Factors Affecting Teachers in the School Systems of the 50 Largest Cities and Selected Suburbs Enrolling 6,000 Pupils or More." Chicago, Illinois, 1967. Available from ERIC, Document #ED 011 880.

1355. _____. "A Survey of Personnel Welfare Provisions for Public School Teachers in Public School Systems Enrolling 6,000 or More Pupils." Chicago, Illinois, 1966. Available from ERIC, Document #ED 010 774.

1356. Glancy, Barbara Jean. "Children's Interracial Fiction: An Unselective Bibliography; Curricular Viewpoints Series." Washington, D.C., 1969. Available from ERIC, Document #ED 037 509.

1357. Goldman, Louis A., et al. "Pensions for Teachers: A Practical Handbook on Pensions and Related Subjects for Teachers in Public Schools and Municipal Colleges of the City of New York." Chicago, Illinois, 1964. Available from ERIC, Document #ED 010 773.

1358. Hixon, Richard A. "A Position Paper (on Collective Bargaining)." Washington, D.C., 1968. Available from ERIC, Document #ED 024 372.

1359. Leahy, Mary Lee. "A New Tenure Act; Mimeograph Monograph Series." Chicago, Illinois, 1966. Available from ERIC, Document #ED 019 748.

1360. Masciantonio, Rudolf. "Latin for the Disadvantaged." Washington, D.C., 1969. Available from ERIC, Document #ED 038 882.

1361. Megel, Carl J., et al. "Representing Today's Teachers: The Story of the American Federation of Teachers in 1963–1964."

Chicago, Illinois, 1964. WSU AFT Collection, unprocessed material.

1362. Oliver, John. "Survey of Teachers' Salaries in U.S. Public School Systems." Washington, D.C., 1969. WSU AFT Collection, Research Department, unnumbered box.

1363. Reuter, George S., Jr. "Fiscal Independence *versus* Fiscal Dependence of School Boards: A Key to Better Schools." Chicago, Illinois, 1960. WSU AFT Collection, Miscellaneous Publications, A–L.

1364. ———. "Historical Justification for Federal Aid to Education." Chicago, Illinois, 1960. WSU AFT Collection, unprocessed material.

1365. ———. "Reforms Needed in the Selection of Textbooks." Chicago, Illinois, 1962. WSU AFT Collection, Miscellaneous Publications, M–R.

1366. ———. "A Sample Study of the 1961 Legislative Goals of Certain State Federations of Teachers." Chicago, Illinois, 1961. WSU AFT Collection, Series I, Box 70.

1367. ———. "School Dropouts and Quality Education." Chicago, Illinois, 1964. WSU AFT Collection, Series I, Box 30.

1368. ———. "A Selected Bibliography Concerning Merit Rating." Chicago, Illinois, 1962. WSU AFT Collection, Series V, Box 6.

1369. ———. "The Teacher and Grievance Procedures." Chicago, Illinois, 1962. WSU AFT Collection, Series I, Box 12.

1370. Schnaufer, Pete. "Three Characters in Search of an AFT Building Representatives Handbook." Chicago, Illinois, 1966. WSU AFT Collection, Miscellaneous Publications, R–Z.

1371. ———. "The Uses of Teacher Power." Chicago, Illinois, 1966. Available from ERIC, Document #ED 011 519.

1372. Schwager, Sidney. "An Analysis of the Evaluation of the More Effective Schools Program Conducted by the Center for Urban Education." Chicago, Illinois, 1967. Available from ERIC, Document #ED 014 526.

1373. Selden, David. "Evaluate Teachers? QuEST Papers Series, #4." Washington, D.C., 1969. Available from ERIC, Document #ED 032 271.

1374. _____. "Teacher Workload and Teacher Dropout. QuEST Papers Series, #5." Washington, D.C., 1969. Available from ERIC, Document #ED 032 272.

1375. Sloan, Irving. "The Negro in Modern American History Textbooks: A Study of the Negro in Selected Junior and Senior High History Textbooks as of September, 1966; Curricular Viewpoints Series." Chicago, Illinois, 1966. Available from ERIC, Document #ED 025 546.

1376. United Federation of Teachers. "The United Federation of Teachers Looks at School Decentralization—A Critical Analysis of the Bundy Report with UFT Proposals." New York, New York, 1967. Available from ERIC, Document #ED 016 021.

1970–1978

1377. American Federation of Teachers. "AFT Membership by States and Locals for Membership Years 1973 and 1974." Washington, D.C., 1974. Available from ERIC, Document #ED 097 767.

1378. _____. "AFT–QuEST Consortium Yearbook: Proceedings of the AFT–QuEST Consortium (April 2–6, 1972)." Washington, D.C., 1972. Available from ERIC, Document #ED 073 060.

1379. ———. "AFT–QuEST Consortium Yearbook: Proceedings of the AFT-QuEST Consortium (April 22–26, 1973)." Washington, D.C., 1973. Available from ERIC, Document #ED 080 519.

1380. ———. "Agreement Between the Board of Regents of Education and the Rhode Island College Staff Association of the AFT." Washington, D.C., 1976. Available from ERIC, Document #ED 122 680.

1381. ———. "Constitution of the AFT." Washington, D.C., 1974. Available from ERIC, Document #ED 096 275.

1382. "Convention Report 1978." Washington, D.C., 1978. Available from ERIC, Document #ED 162 975.

1383. "In Search of Excellence: Questions and Answers about the AFT." Washington, D.C., 1978. WSU Vertical File Material.

1384. ———. "A National Design for the Elementary School." Washington, D.C., 1973. Available from ERIC, Document #ED 083 200.

1385. ———. "A National Design for the High School." Washington, D.C., 1973. Available from ERIC, Document #ED 083 201.

1386. ———. "A National Design for the Middle School." Washington, D.C., 1973. Available from ERIC, Document #ED 083 199.

1387. ———. "Paraprofessionals in the Union: A Matter of Pride." Washington, D.C., 1978. WSU Vertical File Material.

1388. ———. "Putting Early Childhood and Day Care Services into the Public Schools: The Position of the American Federation of Teachers and An Action Plan for Promoting It." Washington, D.C., 1976. Available from ERIC, Document #ED 133 057.

1389. American Federation of Teachers. "Teachers' Centers: A

New Voice for Teachers in Teacher Education Reform." Washington, D.C., 1978. Available from ERIC, Document #ED 162 978.

1390. ———. "Teaching as a Career." Washington, D.C., 1973. Available from ERIC, Document #ED 098 192.

1391. Aran, Kenneth, et al. "The History of Black Americans: A Study Guide and Curriculum Outline." Washington, D.C., 1972. Available from ERIC, Document #ED 076 734.

1392. ———. Puerto Rican History and Culture: A Study Guide and Curriculum Outline." Washington, D.C., 1973. Available from ERIC, Document #ED 088 760.

1393. Bhaerman, Robert D. "American Federation of Teachers' Statement on Vertical Staffing." Washington, D.C., 1971. Available from ERIC, Document #ED 053 072.

1394. ———. "New Currents in Education: A Preliminary Review. QuEST Papers Series, #10." Washington, D.C., 1970. Available from ERIC, Document #ED 043 569.

1395. ———. "An Open Letter to Deans of Teacher Education and Directors of Teacher Certification on Performance-Based Teacher Education/Certification (Is It a "No Exit" Syndrome?). QuEST Papers Series, #14." Washington, D.C., 1974. Available from ERIC, Document #ED 090 169.

1396. ———. "A Paradigm for Accountability. QuEST Paper 12." Washington, D.C., 1970. Available from ERIC, Document #ED 041 870.

1397. ———. "Response to Lessinger: The Great Day of Judgment." Washington, D.C., 1970. Available from ERIC, Document #ED 045 568.

1398. ———. "A Study Outline on Differentiated Staffing. QuEST Report 2." Washington, D.C., 1970. Available from ERIC, Document #ED 046 865.

1399. Brown, George I. "Affectivity, Classroom Climate, and Teaching." Washington, D.C., 1971. Available from ERIC, Document #ED 054 053.

1400. Gaskie, John J. and Margaret F. Gaskie. "Striving Toward Dialogue. A National Forum on Educational Accountability. Denver, Colorado, 1975." Washington, D.C., 1975. Available from ERIC, Document #ED 116 358.

1401. Kemble, Eugenia. "At Last, Teacher Centers That Are Really for Teachers: A Discussion of the New Federal Teacher Center Legislation and What It Can Mean to Teachers." Washington, D.C., 1978. Available from ERIC, Document #ED 162 977.

1402. _____. "Our National Education and Work Policy: Pitfalls and Possibilities. A Position Paper of the AFT Task Force on Educational Issues." Washington, D.C., 1977. Available from ERIC, Document #ED 149 012.

1403. Myers, Donald A. "A Bibliography on Professionalization and Collective Bargaining." Washington, D.C., 1974. Available from ERIC, Document #ED 098 186.

1404. Oliver, John. "Survey of Teachers' Salaries in U.S. Public School Systems. With Statistical Appendix." Washington, D.C., 1975. Available from ERIC, Document #ED 111 779.

1405. Rauth, Marilyn. "The Education for All Handicapped Children Act (P.L. 94-142): Preserving Both Children's and Teachers' Rights." Washington, D.C., 1978. Available from ERIC, Document #ED 162 979.

1406. _____. "A Guide to Understanding the Education for All Handicapped Children Act (P.L. 94-142). Washington, D.C., 1978. Available from ERIC, Document #ED 162 980.

1407. _____. "Mainstreaming: A River to Nowhere or a Promising Current? A Special Report to the AFT Task Force on Educational Issues." Washington, D.C., 1978. Available from ERIC, Document #ED 162 976.

1408. Ryan, Kevin. "Survival Is Not Enough: Overcoming the Problems of Beginning Teachers." Washington, D.C., 1974. Available from ERIC, Document #ED 090 200.

1409. Selden, David. "The State of Our Union." Washington, D.C., 1970. Available from ERIC, Document #ED 043 592.

1410. Sherman, Robert R. "Tenure under Attack: Myth and Fact in the Tenure Debate." Washington, D.C., 1971. Available from ERIC, Document #ED 073 114.

1411. _____. "What Is Tenure? A Critical Explanation. An AFT QuEST Report." Washington, D.C., 1973. Available from ERIC, Document #ED 072 037.

1412. Sloan, Irving. "The American Labor Movement in Modern History and Government Textbooks." Washington, D.C., 1974. Available from ERIC, Document #ED 088 789.

1413. _____. "The Negro in Modern American History Text-books, Fourth Edition: An Examination and Analysis of the Treatment of Black History in Selected Junior and Senior High School Level History Textbooks, as of September, 1972; Curricular Viewpoints Series." Washington, D.C., 1972. Available from ERIC, Document #ED 069 838.

1414. _____. "The Treatment of Black Americans in Current Encyclopedias, First Edition; Curricular Viewpoints Series." Washington, D.C., 1970. Available from ERIC, Document #ED 090 113.

1415. Sperling, John G. "Collective Bargaining and the Teaching-Learning Process. QuEST Paper 11." Washington, D.C., 1970. Available from ERIC, Document #ED 043 568.

1416. Stern, Marjorie, ed. "Changing Sexist Practices in the Classroom: Women in Education." Washington, D.C., 1972. Available from ERIC, Document #ED 092 466.

1417. Ward, James G. and Diane Maldonado. "Language and Children: The Issues in Bilingual Education." Washington, D.C., 1978. WSU Vertical File Material.

V. ARCHIVAL MATERIAL

1418. American Federation of Teachers. *Records, 1914–1978.*
Records of the national federation headquarters include the files of the President's Office (1914–1967), of the Executive Council (1930–1970), charters of the state and local federations (1916–1968), defense cases (1930–1967), memoranda and mimeographed material (1921–1967), and miscellaneous historical papers (including unpublished manuscripts by Freeland G. Stecker, first AFT Secretary-Treasurer). The collection also contains a set of financial ledgers for the years 1916–1961 and proceedings of the annual conventions. Altogether, these materials cover nearly every phase of union activity up to the mid-1960s. *225 linear feet.*

1419. Archdiocesan Teachers Federation. *Papers, 1967–1975.*
The records of Local 1700 include correspondence, financial statements, and printed material. *1 linear foot.*

1420. Borchardt, Selma. *Papers, 1911–1967 (predominantly 1920–1962).*
Borchardt was AFT Washington representative and vice president from 1924 to 1962. Her files cover not only issues crucial to the national union, but also her involvement with the World Federation of Education Associations and with Local 8, Washington, D.C. Borchardt was an important advocate of federal aid to education, child labor legislation, equal rights for women, and other reforms. *100 linear feet.*

1421. DeShetler, Irwin. *Papers, 1933–1971.*
DeShetler was for many years AFL–CIO Assistant Regional Director in California. His papers include several files of correspondence concerning the AFT, 1956–1965. *60 linear feet.*

1422. East Detroit Federation of Teachers. *Records, 1953–1964.*
This collection reflects more the affairs of the Michigan and Macomb County federations than the business of Local 698. *4 linear feet.*

1423. Ecorse Federation of Teachers. *Records, 1960-1965.*
Correspondence, clippings, membership lists, and reports of this suburban Detroit Local 1425. *1 linear foot.*

1424. Elder, Arthur. *Papers, 1921-1953.*
Elder was a vice president of the national AFT and an officer of the Michigan and Detroit federations. The collection is particularly important for the early history of the Detroit local. Elder's papers also reflect his position as director of the University of Michigan Workers Education Service. *10 linear feet.*

1425. Hamilton, Henry. *Papers, 1966-1969.*
Hamilton was vice president of the Michigan Federation of Teachers. His papers include files on Warren (Michigan) Local 1555 and the conflict between the Detroit Federation of Teachers' Local 231 and locals in surrounding communities. *17 linear feet.*

1426. Hamtramck Federation of Teachers. *Records, 1957-1963.*
A small collection of correspondence and printed materials from the suburban Detroit Local 1052. *1 linear foot.*

1427. Herrick, Mary J. *Papers, 1932-1966.*
Correspondence, reports, and clippings relating to AFT organizational activity and the union research department, which Herrick headed in the thirties. *2 linear feet.* See also the Citizens' Schools Committee Collection at the Chicago Historical Society.

1428. Jablonower, Joseph. *Papers, 1912-1965 (predominantly 1930-1950).*
Jablonower was an officer and leading member of TUCNY, Local 5, the New York Teachers Guild, and the UFT. His papers include correspondence and records of other New York locals. *4 linear feet.*

1429. Jones, Dorothy. *Oral history transcript, 1968.*
Topics include the UFT, the Ocean Hill-Brownsville dispute, and the Black Caucus of the AFT. *30 pages.*

1430. Kansas City (Missouri) Federation of Teachers. *Records, 1943–1977.*
The records of Local 691 include correspondence, financial records, reports, scrapbooks, and printed material. *26 linear feet.*

1431. Koch, Lucien. *Papers, 1938–1965 (predominantly 1948–1952).*
Koch was an educator and labor leader. He was associated with Commonwealth College (AFT Local 194) from 1923 until 1935. A few of his files from the late thirties and forties reflect back on these years. *4 linear feet.*

1432. Lane, Layle. *Papers, 1940–1969.*
Lane was a member of the American Federation of Teachers' Committee on Democratic Human Relations. The papers include legal briefs, clippings, pamphlets, and speeches. *0.5 linear foot.*

1433. Linville, Henry R. *Papers, 1912–1941.*
Linville was the first president of TUCNY, Local 5. His papers include correspondence, financial reports, and miscellaneous material on the New York local, the national AFT, and the *American Teacher. 2 linear feet.*

1434. McGhee, Rosa. *Papers, 1966–1967.*
The papers include correspondence and reports, and deal with AFT vice presidential activities, and the Southern Regional Caucus. *0.5 linear foot.*

1435. McGough, Mary. *Oral history transcript, 1970.*
The St. Paul Federation of Teachers is discussed in this interview. *90 pages.*

1436. Maki, Eleanor. *Oral history transcript, 1970.*
Topics include the AFT in the 1930s and 1940s. *30 pages.*

1437. Michigan Federation of Teachers. *Records, 1935–1963.*
Correspondence, minutes, and reports concerning the affairs of the state and national union organization. Substantial material concerns the Detroit Federation of Teachers. *37 linear feet.*

1438. Mills, Jewel. *Papers, 1962-1968.*
Mills was a vice president of the Michigan Federation of Teachers and an officer of Local 1448, Utica, Michigan. His papers include correspondence, minutes, and other records from both organizations. *1 linear foot.*

1439. Nelson, Mercedes. *Papers, 1936-1959.*
A former member of the AFT Executive Board and its Independent Caucus, Ms. Nelson's papers contain material on Minneapolis locals 59 and 238, and the WPA locals of the AFT. *1 linear foot.*

1440. Peck, Raymond. *Papers, 1937-1968.*
Peck was an officer of the Ohio State Federation of Teachers and also an AFT vice president. His papers include correspondence, financial statements, and printed material relating to the organizations. *1.5 linear feet.*

1441. Reuther, May Wolf. *Oral history transcript, 1963.*
An interview dealing with the AFT in the 1930s by the wife of Walter P. Reuther. *22 pages.*

1442. Richard, Zeline. *Oral history transcript, 1969.*
A member of the New Caucus of the AFT, the Detroit Federation of Teachers, and a participant in the Racism in Education Conference (1966). *52 pages.*

1443. Roth, Herrick S. *Papers, 1948-1970.*
Roth has served as an AFT vice president and an officer of both the Denver and Colorado federations. His papers include correspondence, minutes, and reports, chiefly relating to the period 1961-1970. *14 linear feet.* See also the Herrick S. Roth collection at the University of Colorado.

1444. St. Louis Teachers Union. *Records, 1950-1970.*
The files of Local 420 are chiefly from the years 1962-1967. Included are correspondence, minutes, and clippings. *6 linear feet.* See also the collections at the University of Missouri-St. Louis.

1445. St. Paul Federation of Teachers. *Records, 1898-1970.*

The collection includes records of the St. Paul Grade Teachers' Federation (1898–1918), of the Federation of Women Teachers and the Federation of Men Teachers (both 1918–1957), and of the merged Local 28. *4 linear feet.*

1446. San Francisco Federation of Teachers. *Records, 1941–1971.* Most of the collection from Local 61 is from 1956–1969. Included are minutes and general office records. *5 linear feet.*

1447. Sayer, Albert. *Papers, 1936–1965.* Sayer was a member and officer of the New York Teachers Guild and the UFT. His papers include correspondence, clippings, and other printed matter relating to the New York locals. *6 linear feet.*

1448. Smith, Stanton and Nancy. *Papers, 1937–1942.* Nancy Smith was the secretary for the individuals who formed the Progressive Caucus of the AFT in the 1940s. Stanton Smith was a vice president of the AFT. The papers include correspondence, ballots, minutes, proceedings, and rosters. *1.5 linear feet.*

1449. Starr, Mark and Helen. *Papers, 1921–1942.* The Starr Collection is composed of the files of Brookwood Labor College (AFT Local 189), plus additional personal papers of Mark Starr, noted labor educator and journalist. Starr joined the Brookwood staff in 1928 and was associated with the school through the 1930s. The Brookwood campus was closed in 1937. Included in the collection are files of correspondence with AFT leaders. *60 linear feet.*

1450. Stern, Marjorie. *Papers, 1967–1975.* Ms. Stern's papers pertain to her roles as an officer of the San Francisco Federation of Teachers (Local 61), and as a member of the Women's Rights Committee of the AFT. *4 linear feet.*

1451. Toledo Federation of Teachers. *Records, 1933–1968.* The files of Local 250 include correspondence, minutes, financial statements, plus papers relating to professional standards, legislation, and the policies of the Toledo School Board. *35 linear feet.*

1452. Topdahl, Manilla P. *Papers, 1941–1965.*
The papers of the former president of the St. Paul Federation of Teachers Local 28 include clippings, constitutions, leaflets, and correspondence. *0.25 linear foot.*

1453. Wayne State University Federation of Teachers. *Records, 1957–1974.*
The files of Local 1295 include correspondence, organizational and financial records, and printed material. *2 linear feet.*

1454. Weil, Truda. *Papers, 1947–1959.*
Ms. Weil was the Executive Secretary of the original New York Teachers Union and later the New York Teachers Guild. Included in the papers is correspondence with John Dewey. *0.25 linear foot.*

1455. Wheeler, Mary. *Papers, 1938–1967.*
Ms. Wheeler was a vice president of the AFT and president of the West Suburban Teachers Union (Illinois) Local 571. Her papers are mainly the printed records of the local. *2 linear feet.*

OTHER REPOSITORIES

1456. University of California, Los Angeles Library. Los Angeles, California.

Frances R. Eisenberg, *papers, 1946–1958*.

Correspondence, tape recordings, pamphlets, periodicals, photographs, and minutes pertaining to Los Angeles Local 430 of the AFT. *11 linear feet.*

1457. Chicago Historical Society. Chicago, Illinois.

Chicago Teachers' Federation, *records, 1897–1969*.

The CTF was founded in 1897 and affiliated with the Chicago Federation of Labor in 1902. With the founding of the AFT in 1916 the CTF become Local 1. Connections with organized labor were broken a year later when the Chicago School Board passed the Loeb rule, banning union membership for teachers. Although a large proportion of early CTF records have been lost, the collection retains some material from the union period. Of particular significance is the unpublished autobiography of Margaret A. Haley. *39 linear feet.*

1458. _____.

Chicago Teachers Union, *records, 1914–1971*.

The CTU, AFT Local 1, was founded in 1937 by a merger of the Chicago Federation of Men Teachers and the Federation of Women Teachers. Many records of these early federations have been preserved in the collection. As a whole, the collection includes correspondence, minutes, financial records, and union publications. Subjects include the Chicago teachers "revolt" of 1933, representation elections, contract bargaining, and educational and municipal reform. *63 linear feet.*

1459. _____.

Citizens' Schools Committee, *records, 1911–1972*.

A collection of correspondence, minutes, and reports of a reform group which was closely allied with the AFT locals in Chicago. Included are the papers of Mary J. Herrick, the founder of the organization and a vice president of the AFT. *20 linear feet, 21 volumes.* See also the Mary J. Herrick collection at Wayne State University.

213

1460. _____.
Lillian Herstein, *papers, 1920-1958.*
Herstein was an officer of the Chicago Federation of Women
High School Teachers and of the Chicago Teachers Union.
1 linear foot.

1461. University of Colorado Libraries, Western Historical Collections. Boulder, Colorado.
Herrick S. Roth, *papers, 1950-1970.*
Correspondence, reports, minutes, court cases, and convention material pertaining to the AFT during the 1960s and 1970s.
31 linear feet. See also the Herrick S. Roth collection at Wayne
State University.

1462. Cornell University, Labor Management Documentation
Center. Ithaca, New York.
Teachers Union of the City of New York, *records, 1921-1965.*
The files of old Local 5 include material on academic freedom
cases, on proposed legislation, and on the expulsion of the
local from the AFT in 1941. *28 linear feet.*

1463. University of Missouri–St. Louis Library. St. Louis, Missouri.
Paul William Preisler, *papers, 1902-1971.*
Preisler was a labor leader, lawyer, and biochemist. His papers
relate to Local 420, St. Louis, Missouri. *16 linear feet.* See also
the St. Louis Teachers Union collection at Wayne State
University.

1464. _____.
St. Louis Teachers Strike of 1973 Collection.
Correspondence, strike bulletins, flyers, court injunctions,
briefs, and tape-recorded interviews with fifteen principal
figures in the Local 420 strike. *3 linear feet.* See also the St.
Louis Teachers Union collection at Wayne State University.

1465. Oregon Historical Society Library. Portland, Oregon.
Portland Federation of Teachers, *records, 1919, 1935-1974.*
Correspondence, membership rolls, bulletins, AFT charters
and minutes. Information on civil rights, school financing,
salaries. *3 linear feet.*

1466. University of Oregon Library. Eugene, Oregon.
Jerome Davis, *papers, 1915–1963.*
Correspondence, diaries, and other papers of the AFT president (1936–1938) and educator, including records pertaining
to Davis's suit against the Curtis Publishing Company (1939–
1950). *17 linear feet.* See also the Jerome Davis collection
at the Franklin D. Roosevelt Library.

1467. Franklin D. Roosevelt Library. Hyde Park, New York.
Jerome Davis, *papers, 1912–1962.*
A small portion of Davis's correspondence in this collection
relates to the AFT. *5 linear feet.* See also the Jerome Davis
collection at the University of Oregon Library.

1468. Stanford University Library. Stanford, California.
Guido Hugo Marx, *papers, 1901–1949.*
Marx was a professor of mechanical engineering at Stanford
University. His papers include correspondence, pamphlets,
clippings, reprints, biographical and autobiographical ma-
terial relating to the AFT in California. *2 linear feet.*

1469. Temple University, Urban Archives. Philadelphia, Penn-
sylvania.
Mary Foley Grossman, *papers, 1934–1941.*
Grossman was secretary-treasurer and a vice president of the
AFT and president of Local 192, Philadelphia. Her collection
includes correspondence and printed materials. *5 linear feet.*

1470. _____.
Philadelphia Teachers Union, *records, 1935–1955.*
The Philadelphia Teachers Union was Local 192 until expelled
from the AFT because of alleged Communist domination. The
records include correspondence, defense cases, financial
records and printed materials. *8 linear feet.*

1471. University of Washington Library. Seattle, Washington.
Arthur F. Broetje, *papers, 1934–1966.*
Broetje was president of Local 336, Bremerton, Washington.
His papers concern the local, the state federation, and the city
and state labor councils of the AFT. *4.5 linear feet.*

1472. _____.
Local 401, University of Washington Teachers Union, *records, 1937–1948.*
Correspondence, minutes, and financial records. *1 linear foot.*

1473. _____.
Elmer Miller, *papers, 1931–1966.*
Miller was president of Local 200, Seattle, and of the Washington State Federation. *15 linear feet.*

1474. State Historical Society of Wisconsin. Madison, Wisconsin.
Madison Federation of Teachers, *records, 1930–1951.*
The records of Local 223 include correspondence, printed materials, and miscellaneous files. *2 linear feet.*

1475. _____.
Wisconsin Federation of Teachers, *records, 1939–1951.*
The collection includes correspondence, minutes, and financial statements. *1 linear foot.*

Note: Numbers refer to bibliographic entries.

Academic freedom, 12, 169, 222, 267, 312, 383, 386, 468, 886
Accountability, 1014, 1095, 1102, 1176, 1373, 1396
Addams, Jane, 7, 116, 1296
Affirmative action: AFT policy, 979, 1008
AFL affiliation. See Teachers' unions: AFL affiliation
AFL-CIO: Council of Scientific, Professional and Cultural Employees (SPACE), 867; history of, 1270; Industrial Union Department, 638, 739; merger of, 322
AFL-CIO affiliation. See Teachers' unions: AFL-CIO affiliation
AFT: archival collections, 1160; constitutions, 1309, 1332; contracts, 1339; history, 1-4, 17, 63, 68, 70, 93, 110, 119, 162, 167, 181, 261, 289, 510, 1269, 1278, 1284, 1286; internal organization, 127, 232; objectives, 608, 738, 920; philosophy and programs, 34, 490-92, 1316, 1330; political action, 453, 1118, 1190, 1227, 1280. See also Local 1 (Chicago Teachers Federation), history; Teachers' unions, history.
Agency shop, 933
Aid to education. See Federal aid to education; Parochial schools: public funds for busing; Tuition tax credit
American Federation of Labor. See AFL
American Federation of Teachers. See AFT
Anchorage (Alaska) local. See Local 1175
Anti-Communism. See Communism and Communists
Anti-Semitism, 873
Anti-strike legislation. See Taylor Law
Associate Teachers League of New Orleans. See Local 36
Atlanta Public School Teachers Association. See Local 89

Balboa (Panama Canal Zone) local. See Local 227
Berkeley (Calif.) locals. See Local 1078; Local 1570
Bilingual education, 1188

Black Mountain Workers' College, 356
Blacks in teachers' unions: AFT desegregation of locals, 549, 468; AFT membership, 329, 782; black locals in Louisiana, 532; dissatisfaction with AFT, 826. See also Local 27; Local 428
Borchardt, Selma, 252, 1420; views, 323-26, 477-79
Boston Teachers Alliance, 914
Boston Teachers Union, 914
Bremerton (Wash.) local. See Local 336
Brookwood Labor College. See Local 189
Buffalo Industrial Teachers' Association. See Local 39
Buffalo (N.Y.) teachers' strikes, 531

California State Federation, 249
Censorship, 616, 801, 832
Chattanooga (Tenn.) local. See Local 246; Local 428
Chicago Art Institute. See Faculty unions: Chicago Art Institute
Chicago City College. See Faculty unions: Chicago City College
Chicago (Ill.) locals. See Local 1; Local 199; Local 1700
Chicago Teachers Federation. See Local 1
Chicago (Ill.) teachers' strike, 420
Chicago Teachers Union. See Local 1
Child welfare, 333, 345, 1028
CIO affiliation. See Teachers' unions: CIO affiliation
City University (New York City). See Faculty unions: City University
Civil rights movement, 691, 760, 831, 908. See also Integration, racial
Class size, 712, 747, 1259
Cleveland Federation of Labor, 179
Cleveland (Ohio) local. See Local 279
Cleveland Teachers Federation, 211
Cleveland (Ohio) teachers' unions: court victory of, 177; firings, 140, 146
Cogen, Charles: AFT philosophy and program, 705, 810, 813; election as AFT president, 639, 647, 668, 761, 955; views, 665-67, 678, 729

Collective bargaining, 537, 544, 564, 629, 665, 734, 808, 828, 870, 1261; administrators' role in, 685; AFT policy toward, 21, 34, 49, 51, 58; opposition to, 735; and professionalism, 876; union size factor in, 156; work stoppages, 637. See also Faculty unionization: collective bargaining

Colleges: unionization of. See Faculty unionization

Commonwealth College (Mena, Ark.), 47, 213, 259, 433, 452

Communism and Communists, 25, 310-11, 327, 556; expulsion from AFT, 45, 341, 450; issue of, 263, 316, 336, 350, 393, 423, 451, 498, 1288; use of Fifth Amendment, 592, 626. See also Local 5; Local 61; Local 192; Local 401; Local 430; Local 453; Local 537; Totalitarianism

Community control, 1013. See also Ocean Hill-Brownsville

Comprehensive Program for American Schools (COMPAS), 1035, 1246

Compulsory arbitration, 588

Congress of Industrial Organizations. See CIO

Council Bluffs (Iowa) local. See Local 738

Counts, George: educational programs, 27, 340; expulsion of communists and fascists, 341

Davis, Jerome, 346-49, 353-54, 1466-67; college unionization, 351; communism issue, 350; Yale dismissal, 309, 331, 440, 445, 454, 473, 1313

Day care, 1077, 1189. See also Pre-school education

Decentralization, 923; Detroit (Mich.), 48, 1048; Los Angeles (Calif.) and Washington (D.C.), 48; New York (N.Y.), 38, 40, 48, 791, 798, 803, 822, 927, 930, 976, 1376. See also Community control; Ocean Hill-Brownsville; New York City teachers' strikes

Democracy and education, 11

Depression: effect on education, 405, 430

Desegregation of schools: New York City, 62; northern states, 824. See also Integration, racial

Detroit Federation of Teachers, 1047, 1422

Detroit (Mich.) schools: race relations in, 539; teachers' strikes in, 19, 1001

Dewey, John, 519, 530; criticism of, 148; educational philosophy of, 96-97, 580, 977; on teachers and labor unions, 99, 366; on vocational education, 98

Disadvantaged children, education of, 813. See also More Effective Schools program

Discipline, classroom, 712. See also Violence in schools

Discrimination. See Handicapped teachers, rights of; Integration, Radical; Women

Dissent, rank and file, 390

Eau Claire (Wis.) local. See Local 696

Education: reform in, 718; role of television in, 634, 1327

Educational freedom, 8

Educational innovations. See Instructional technology; Performance contracting; Voucher plans

Educational programs, 27, 30, 46, 55, 523-24. See also More Effective Schools (MES); Progressive education movement; Quality Educational Standards in Teaching (QuEST)

Elder, Arthur, 1424

Employer-employee relations, 33, 56

Equal Rights Amendment, 984

Equal salary issue (men & women), 290

Faculty unionization, 35, 214, 225, 351-52, 380, 465, 488, 589, 781, 807, 823, 847, 853, 855, 872, 874, 883, 1003-5, 1065, 1108, 1153, 1232, 1248-50, 1283; by American Association of University Professors, 1022; in California, 804; and collective bargaining, 71, 72, 1018, 1034, 1096, 1113; in New York State, 880; of teaching assistants, 698, 1131

Faculty unions: Chicago Art Institute, 700; Chicago City College, 943; City University (New York City), 1158; Philadelphia Community College (Local 2026), 1060; Rhode Island College, 1380; Saint John's University, 799, 836, 859, 916-18; San Francisco State College (Local 1352), 66, 941, 1023; State University of New York (SUNY) (Local 2190), 1230; University of Connecticut, 998; University of Delaware, 1172; University of Washington (Local 401), 525; Wayne State University Federation of Teachers, 1453

Fascism. *See* Totalitarianism

Federal aid to education, 323-24, 379, 403, 474, 477-79, 633, 635, 736, 800, 1092, 1364; to parochial schools, 538, 664; to private schools, 475

Financing of education, 200, 347, 400. *See also* Local 1 (Chicago Teachers Federation); Federal aid to education; Tuition tax credit; Voucher plans

Fulton County (Ga.) local. *See* Local 183

Gary (Ind.) local. *See* Local 4

Goggin, Catherine, 135; founding of Chicago Teachers Federation, 111

Gompers, Samuel: and teacher unionization, 112, 911; views on education, 183

Grievance procedures, 1097, 1369

Haley, Margaret A., 116-17, 135, 139; criticism of, 148; views on education, 114, 183

Hamtramck (Mich.) teachers' strike, 688, 693

Handicapped teachers, rights of, 1147

Health benefits, 343, 578

Herrick, Mary J., 1427

Illinois Federation of Teachers, 1090-91, 1245

Instructional technology, 1180

Integration, racial, 601, 614, 1152, 1272; AFL-CIO policy, 601; AFT policy, 553, 563, 1046, 1128, 1337; UFT policy, 929. *See also* Affirmative action; Blacks in teachers' unions; Civil rights movement; Racial distribution of teachers

Jacksonville (Fla.) local. *See* Local 516

Kenosha (Wis.) local. *See* Local 577

Ketchikan (Alaska) local. *See* Local 868

Kuenzli, Irvin R., 552

Labor affiliation. *See* Teachers' unions: AFL affiliation, AFL-CIO affiliation, CIO affiliation, labor affiliation

Labor colleges. *See* Black Mountain Workers' College; Commonwealth College; Local 189, Brookwood Labor College; Sweet Briar College Southern Summer School for Women

Labor relations. *See* Employer-employee relations

Lefkowitz, Abraham, 237-41, 404

Linville, Henry R., 243-4, 402, 455, 1433; criticism of, 899

Local 1 (Chicago Teachers Federation): dismissals in, 100-101; history of, 28, 32, 103-104, 120, 162, 184, 189-90, 1262, 1457; labor affiliation, 147, 151, 160; strike by, 157; tax assessment dispute, 7, 88, 91, 102, 108, 135, 145, 173-74

Local 1 (Chicago Teachers Union), 59, 415, 460, 497, 612, 663, 1458

Local 2 (UFT, New York City), 750

Local 3 (Philadelphia, Pa.), 733

Local 4 (Gary, Ind.), 61, 614, 753

Local 5 (New York City), 125, 313, 362, 389, 401, 402, 406, 455, 1433, 1462; and communist dispute, 76, 337, 404, 412, 422, 469, 472; expulsion of, 68, 336, 370, 424, 432, 434, 457, 463, 690, 899; history of, 6, 125, 188; and rating system dispute, 321. *See also* New York Teachers' League

Local 6 (Washington, D.C.), 963, 1236

Local 8 (Washington, D.C.), 215

Local 24 (New York City), 314

Local 27 (Washington, D.C.), 251

Local 36 (New Orleans, La.), 106

Local 39 (Buffalo, N.Y.), 372

Local 52 (Memphis, Tenn.), 245, 265-66

Local 59 (Minneapolis, Minn.), 542, 613

Local 61 (San Francisco, Calif.), 255, 264, 339, 438, 525, 957, 1446

Local 89 (Atlanta, Ga.), 196, 224

Local 111 (Portland, Oreg.), 279, 520

Local 183 (Fulton County, Ga.), 297

Local 189 (Brookwood Labor College, Katonah, N.Y.), 57, 220, 226, 230, 240, 256, 270, 303, 338, 627, 882, 1223, 1449; defense by John Dewey, 216; dismissal of Arthur W. Calhoun, 206; dispute with AFL, 204

Local 192 (Philadelphia, Pa.), 336-37, 370, 424, 432, 434

Local 197 (Providence, R.I.), 231

Local 199 (Chicago, Ill.), 236, 304

Local 200 (Seattle, Wash.), 887

Local 207 (Savannah, Ga.), 223

Local 215 (San Francisco Administrators' Federation), 437

Local 227 (Balboa, C.Z.), 574

Local 238 (Minneapolis, Minn.), 613

Local 246 (Chattanooga, Tenn.), 447

Local 250 (Toledo, Ohio), 481, 622

Local 252 (Milwaukee, Wis.), 720

Local 279 (Cleveland, Ohio), 400, 567, 569

Local 336 (Bremerton, Wash.), 583
Local 401 (University of Washington), 525, 1472
Local 420 (Saint Louis, Mo.), 374, 1444
Local 428 (Chattanooga, Tenn.), 526
Local 430 (Los Angeles, Calif.), 525
Local 453 (New York City), 457
Local 516 (Jacksonville, Fla.), 385
Local 527 (New Orleans, La.), 1142
Local 537 (New York City), 336-37, 370, 424, 432, 434, 457
Local 557 (Kenosha, Wis.), 565
Local 696 (Eau Claire, Wis.), 566, 725
Local 738 (Council Bluffs, Iowa), 582
Local 833 (West New York, N.J., Federation of Teachers), 573
Local 868 (Ketchikan, Alaska), 476
Local 930, (Pawtucket, R.I.), 598
Local 1078 (Berkeley Federation of Teachers), 997, 1012
Local 1085 (Taylor, Mich.), 695
Local 1087 (Pocatello, Idaho), 576
Local 1175 (Anchorage, Alaska), 625
Local 1352 (San Francisco State College), 66, 941, 1023
Local 1520 (Cincinnati Federation of Teachers), 1029
Local 1570 (Berkeley, Calif.), 698
Local 1700 (Chicago, Ill.), 940
Local 1931 (San Diego Community College), 978
Local 2026 (Philadelphia Community College), 1060
Local 2190 (State University of New York), 1230
Local 3211 (San Ysidro, Calif.), 1026
Local 3479 (Valdez, Alaska), 1239
Loeb, Jacob M.: views on Chicago Federation of Labor, 128
Loeb rule, 28, 32, 82, 84-87, 90, 100, 118, 178; AFT opposition to, 175-76. See also Local 1 (Chicago Teachers Federation)
Los Angeles (Calif.) local. See Local 430
Loyalty oaths, 595, 901, 1328; in Mass., 376; at University of Florida, 1220. See also Lusk laws
Lusk laws, 239, 244, 246, 295; J. Dewey, 307

McDowell, Mary, 116
Megel, Carl, 699, 704
Memphis (Tenn.) local. See Local 52
Merit rating, 321, 330, 505, 517, 529, 569, 680, 716, 1315, 1368

Michigan Federation of Teachers, 1437
Militancy, 672, 686, 708-9, 726, 761, 894, 912, 947, 970, 975, 1042, 1126, 1174, 1177. See also Strikes, teachers'
Milwaukee (Wis.) local. See Local 252
Minneapolis (Minn.) local. See Local 59, Local 238
Minneapolis (Minn.) teachers' strikes, 533, 588
Minnesota Federation of Teachers, 218
More Effective Schools program, 649, 921, 962, 1166, 1258, 1345, 1372
Muste, A. J., 44. See also Local 189, Brookwood Labor College

National Education Association. See NEA
NEA: AFL-CIO view of, 545; AFT disaffiliation with (N.Y.), 1143-46; collective bargaining by, 67, 1106; comparison with AFT, 232, 508, 659, 664, 681, 683, 721, 732, 744, 756, 772-73, 776, 789-90, 795, 816, 827, 851-52, 888, 890-91, 910, 919, 1049, 1055, 1072, 1140, 1151, 1268, 1295; "conscripted" membership, 717; effect of AFT on, 68; election loss to AFT, 673, 1159; labor affiliations of, 50, 170; militancy of, 686; and strikes, 811, 848. See also NEA-AFT, domination of education; NEA-AFT, merger prospects; NEA-AFT, rivalry of
NEA-AFT, domination of education, 1257
NEA-AFT, merger prospects, 50, 710, 724, 825, 830, 850, 875, 879, 892-93, 986, 987, 1010, 1032, 1044, 1080, 1087, 1100, 1110, 1120, 1122, 1139, 1234, 1237; in Flint (Mich.), 786, 1117, 1125; in Los Angeles (Calif.), 1242; in Monroe County (Fla.), 1132; in New York, 1107
NEA-AFT, rivalry of, 36, 64, 187, 210, 285, 509, 660-62, 679, 684, 696, 713, 802, 806, 938, 1212, 1216, 1243; in Cleveland (Ohio), 778; in Dayton (Ohio), 792; in Seattle (Wash.), 278. See also Seattle (Wash.) contract dispute (1928)
Newark (N.J.) teachers' strike, 1150, 1157
New Orleans (La.) local. See Local 36; Local 527
New York City financial crisis (1975), 1170, 1184, 1205
New York City (N.Y.) local. See Local 2; Local 5; Local 24; Local 453; Local 537
New York City teachers' strikes, 23, 54,

73, 74, 657-58, 694, 711, 740, 751-52, 755, 764, 775, 796, 803, 814, 884-85, 904, 935-36, 1116. See also Ocean Hill-Brownsville
New York City teachers' unions, history of, 5-6, 125, 188. See also Local 5: history of; UFT (New York City): history of
New York Teachers' League, 94
Norwalk (Conn.) teachers' strike, 536
No-strike policy (AFT), 227, 300, 500, 504, 551

Ocean Hill-Brownsville dispute, 2, 14, 22, 788, 842, 854, 884, 939, 948, 961, 974. See also Community control; New York City teachers' strikes; UFT (New York City)
Organizing: of non-teaching personnel, 996, 1037, 1098, 1156; of teachers, 1, 10, 30, 144, 199, 1082, 1177. See also Teachers' unions

Paraprofessionals, 980, 1085-86, 1101, 1112, 1154-55, 1177, 1346, 1387
Parochial schools: participation in collective bargaining, 1030; public funds for busing, 548; unionization, 1129. See also Federal aid to education: to parochial schools
Pawtucket (R.I.) local. See Local 930
Pawtucket (R.I.) teachers' strike, 636
Pension plans, 191, 1357
Performance contracting, 862, 1089, 1124
Philadelphia Community College. See Local 2026
Philadelphia (Pa.) locals. See Local 3; Local 192; Local 2026
Pocatello (Idaho) local. See Local 1087
Portland (Oreg.) local. See Local 111
Pre-school education, 1062, 1068, 1388
Professionalism and unionization, 228, 288, 794, 849, 866, 869, 1058, 1164, 1297-98, 1403
Progressive Education Movement, 29, 340
Proposition 13, 1199
Providence (R.I.) local. See Local 197
Puerto Rico teachers' strike, 1240

Quality Educational Standards in Teaching (QuEST) program, 905, 980, 990-92, 1015, 1017, 1039, 1067, 1241, 1340, 1378-79

Racial distribution of teachers, 1187
Racial integration. See Integration, racial
Racism in education, 818, 906
Rating system disputes. See Merit rating
Residency requirements, 1201
Retirement benefits, 369, 480, 570
Rhode Island College. See Faculty unions: Rhode Island College
Right to strike. See Strikes
"Right-to-work" legislation, 1103

Sabbatical leave, 254, 269, 275
Saint John's University. See Faculty unions: Saint John's University
Saint Louis (Mo.) local. See Local 420
Saint Paul Federation of Teachers, 1445
Saint Paul (Minn.) teachers' strike, 518, 527-28
Salaries, 109, 201, 272, 401, 609, 1354, 1362; and race and sex discrimination, 287, 416, 507
Salary cuts, 405, 408, 470
San Diego (Calif.) local. See Local 1931, San Diego Community College
San Francisco (Calif.) locals. See Local 61; Local 215; Local 1352
San Ysidro (Calif.) local. See Local 3211
Savannah (Ga.) local. See Local 207
School administration: AFT position, 20, 153
Seattle (Wash.) contract dispute (1928), 277-78, 281-84
Seattle (Wash.) local. See Local 200
Segregation. See Integration, racial
Selden, David: program, 784; resignation, 1181; views, 643, 813
Sex discrimination, 1416. See also Salaries; Women
Shanker, Albert, 907, 960, 1000, 1009, 1053-54, 1105, 1167, 1212-19, 1247; articles by, 750-51, 929-32, 1183-211; criticism, 1253; imprisonment, 863, 954; President of AFL-CIO Department of Professional Employees, 1162-63; President of AFT, 989; President of UFT, 668; views, 862
State University of New York (SUNY) local. See Local 2190
Strikes, 516, 522, 534, 591, 617, 619-20, 671, 731, 817, 840, 845, 860, 881, 926, 944, 946, 950-52, 1255, 1260, 1276, 1301; as union weapon, 298, 318, 586, 748; effects on students, 966; prevention of, 587; public reaction to, 1293; racial tensions as cause, 885, 1001; "right to

strike," 489, 594, 763. *See also under name of individual city*; No-strike policy; Taylor Law
Students: failing of, 1195; rights of, 909, 942, 1028
Supervisors' locals, 437
Sweet Briar College Southern Summer School for Women, 242

Tax cuts, 1194. *See also* Proposition 13
Taxes. *See* Financing of education
Taylor (Mich.) local. *See* Local 1085
Taylor Law (N.Y.), 796, 833, 880, 889
Teachers: dismissals for union membership, 140, 171, 235, 283; shortage of, 605; unionization and democracy, 123, 129, 149
Teachers aides. *See* Paraprofessionals
Teachers' unions: AFL affiliation, 105, 142, 159, 268, 274; AFL-CIO affiliation, 600, 621, 638, 642; arguments pro and con, 24, 78, 112, 115, 121, 128, 150, 155, 161, 163, 192, 203, 260, 483, 655, 743, 972, 1040; CIO affiliation, 407, 436, 462; history of, 9, 79, 81, 1019, 1274, 1277, 1281, 1294; John Dewey defense on, 217; labor affiliation, 69; membership characteristics of, 16, 815, 1133-34, 1137; in private schools, 1099
Television. *See* Education: role of television
Tenure, 77, 169, 212, 593, 1410-11
Tenure laws, 205, 219, 250, 253, 257, 326, 369, 373, 466, 555, 1359
Testing: Albert Shanker's views on, 1036
Toledo Federation of Teachers, 1451
Toledo (Ohio) local. *See* Local 250
Totalitarianism, 335, 461
Tuition tax credit, 981, 1185, 1213

UFT (New York City), 26, 74, 656, 669, 692, 706-7, 728, 741, 747, 750, 762, 787, 842, 844, 914, 937, 964-65, 1013; collective bargaining strategy, 667, 819; criticism of, 1041; history of, 6, 23, 26, 63; strike policy of, 666. *See also* New York City financial crisis (1975); New York City teachers' strikes; Ocean Hill-Brownsville
Union security clauses, 1252
Unions. *See* Teachers' unions
Union shop, 572
United Federation of Teachers. *See* UFT
U.S. Department of Education, AFT

policy toward establishment of, 124, 995, 1200, 1218-19
University of Connecticut. *See* Faculty unions: University of Connecticut
University of Delaware. *See* Faculty unions: University of Delaware
University of Washington. *See* Faculty unions: University of Washington

Valdez (Alaska) local. *See* Local 3479
Vietnam war: AFT position, 785
Violence in schools, 562, 1148
Vocational education, 98, 372, 547, 1256, 1334
Voucher plans, 1124, 1178-79

Washington (D.C.) locals. *See* Local 6; Local 8; Local 27
Washington (D.C.) schools: teachers strikes, 1043; teachers unionization, 182
Wayne State University Federation of Teachers, 1453
West New York (N.J.) local. *See* Local 833
Wisconsin Summer School for Workers in Industry, 442
Women: discrimination against women teachers, 1059, 1061, 1228, 1416; in labor movement, 43; separate locals for, 418. *See also* Equal Rights Amendment; Equal salary issue
Woodbridge (N.J.) teachers' strike, 805
Work: stoppages, 637; conditions, 243, 793, 1127
Workers, education of, 15, 98, 234. *See also* Black Mountain Workers' College; Commonwealth College; Local 189, Brookwood Labor College; Sweet Briar College Southern Summer School for Women; Vocational education; Wisconsin Summer School for Workers in Industry
World War I: AFT policy, 172
World War II; AFT policy, 365, 429, 484, 543

"Yellow-dog" contracts, 414; Saint Louis (Mo.), 276, 374, 428; Seattle, Wash., 277, 282-83, 375, 435, 456, 887. *See also* Loeb rule; Seattle (Wash.) contract dispute (1928)